Sophie's Journey

Also by Sophie Thurnham

THE GREAT DONKEY TREK

Sophie's Journey

The Story of an Aid Worker in Romania

Sophie Thurnham

Sophie Thurnham

August 1995

WARNER BOOKS

A *Warner* Book

First published in Great Britain by Warner in 1994

Copyright © Sophie Thurnham 1994

A CIP catalogue record for this book
is available from the British Library

ISBN 0 7515 1006 8

Typeset by Hewer Text Composition Services, Edinburgh
Printed and bound in Great Britain by Clays Ltd, St Ives plc

Warner
A division of
Little, Brown and Company (UK) Limited
Brettenham House
Lancaster Place
London WC2 7EN

For

Aileen, Colette, Maureen,
Andrew, Collette and Paddy,
with much love

Contents

Acknowledgements

I would like to thank my parents for their unstinting support for what I was doing in Romania. It meant and it helped a great deal. Thanks to the many Romanians who helped me throughout my travels – your friendliness and generosity touched me deeply.

My apologies to the many volunteers at Yonashen and Podriga whom I failed to mention – most especially Vicki, Jenny and Sam. If I had set out to write about who were the hardest workers, it would have been a very different story, and in trying to keep the book personal, I realize I have not done nearly enough justice to the input of the other volunteers.

On behalf of all of us who were working out there, I'd like to thank the silent army of supporters back home who provided the necessary funds, equipment and supplies for what we were doing – you know who you are.

My thanks to Lis and Tony Farrell for letting me stay in their home whilst writing the book, to Patrick Walsh for his faith and enthusiasm in the project, and to my editors at Little, Brown, Hilary Foakes and Martin Bryant, for liking it and not wanting to change everything in it.

For anyone wondering what became of the animals: Hannibal is now living on a beautiful little farm in Normandy; Georgie is with me in Africa, spending her days chasing lizards and barking at monkeys; and Smeckie and Nipper are still helping keep the Podriga volunteers sane, although the last I heard, Andrew was making preparations for taking them home.

Note

Since Romanian pronunciation can be incomprehensible and the Romanian alphabet contains letters not known in the West, I have spelt many Romanian words and names phonetically. Certain names and places have also been altered so as to respect the privacy of those mentioned.

.... ROUGH JOURNEY ROUTE

⌒⌒⌒ CARPATHIAN MOUNTAINS

Introduction
Searching for the Sword of Truth and Justice

It seems so strange now, looking back on the time before I went to Romania; not because I think I've changed in any great way, but simply because a country that used to mean nothing to me – nothing at all – for a while took over my whole existence. For the first twenty-two years of my life, the only Romanians I'd heard of were Ili Nastase and Nadia Chomeneci. I didn't know who the president was, and I couldn't have placed it accurately on a map. Romania was just part of the Eastern Bloc, well-established before I was born and which I imagined would be thus forever.

When the peaceful revolutions in Eastern Europe began, I found myself fascinated by this country where revolution was not happening. For the first time I learned of the particular harshness of the Romanian regime. Ceauşescu came to mean something to me – the personification of evil, almost too bad to be true, but apparently going strong. The thought of living in such a place was beyond my imagination. Then the massacres of Timishoara happened, with all the rumours of tens of thousands being killed, and I remember sitting riveted to the television as Ceauşescu's regime crumbled so suddenly.

I'm almost ashamed that the bloodshed of revolution

didn't shock me more, but I remember feeling exhilarated by it all – here was a war worth fighting. Half of me wanted to grab a gun and fly out to join the Romanian people in their fight against the Securitate snipers. All those airy words like freedom and democracy actually meant something for once; good was defeating evil, and it felt marvellous.

At the time I had just returned from a solo adventure around the Mediterranean and was trying to write my first travel book. Friends were already pestering me about where I would go next, and suddenly my mind was made up – Romania. I'd witness a nation's awakening – twenty million individuals suddenly fulfilling their dreams, speaking freely, taking charge of their own destinies. I became completely carried away by the romance of revolution; history was in the making, and I wanted to be a part of it all.

Over the following year, holed up in the English Lake District trying to write, I immersed myself in articles about what had happened in Romania. Nicolae Ceauşescu emerged as the most despicable tyrant. He had based his regime on that of North Korea with himself at the head of a huge personality cult backed by a ruthless secret police. In the 1970s he embarked on a massive industrialization programme, incurring huge national debts and forcing what had been a predominantly peasant population into the cities by simply destroying their homes, bulldozing through the plains of southern Romania to create massive collective farms where once had stood villages. In the 1980s Ceauşescu had determinedly paid back the foreign debt, infuriating foreign banks by sending them shipments of grain and cattle in lieu of cash. The Romanian people were kept in virtual starvation, with meat an unheard of luxury in the cities, while he and his top circle of sycophants lived off produce from the farms and greenhouses at his many palaces. He was particularly fond of mango for breakfast.

Ceauşescu dreamed of doubling Romania's population by the year 2000. He was an uneducated man, purported not even to be able to write coherently, and in his naive beliefs he thought that a country's wealth was directly related to the size of its workforce. He had therefore set about a horrendous programme of child production, banning all contraception, imposing penalties on the childless and regularly screening women to ensure against backstreet abortions.

Soon after the revolution the international media discovered Romania's orphanages. With the destruction of the old peasant communities and their family support networks, women stuck in tower blocks in grim industrial cities had evidently not been able to cope with the children they were being forced to produce. There had been no social welfare system to help out and a man's salary was simply not enough to feed a large family. The result was an estimated 140,000 children in care. They were found in conditions which shocked the globe, stuck in institutions resembling concentration camps. The images of starving, filthy babies crammed into row upon row of cots prompted Western Europe and the United States to send in emergency relief teams. I was one of the many who contacted the Red Cross offering to go and work at an orphanage, saying I'd scrub floors, do anything that could make a difference, but I was told that unless I was a doctor or nurse I had nothing to offer. I had to be content with hoping that as part of my travels I could visit some of the institutions and by writing about them I could perhaps make a contribution to change.

The orphanages only strengthened my impression of the poor Romanian people having lived through a total nightmare. I couldn't wait to actually meet Romanians and see how the new freedom had changed things. With *perestroika* breaking new boundaries in the Soviet Union, and Latvia and Estonia making bids for independence in the Baltics, the feeling continued that something tremendously exciting was taking place behind what had been the Iron Curtain. Brave men and women were shaping history according to the best principles of mankind, fighting tyranny and corruption with nothing but the sword of truth and justice.

I soon learnt. Within a few weeks of arriving in Romania I was completely disillusioned; I'd never come across such racism, such snobbery, such callousness. I nearly left the country for good. But, desperate to understand, I persisted, and it was worth it. I ended up staying for one and a half years, most of it spent in an isolated corner of northern Moldavia where I attempted to make a personal contribution to Romanian change. In historical terms it counted for nothing, yet I now realize that a true revolution probably means this rather than picking up a rifle and taking a pot shot at a sniper.

Democracy and freedom are flowery, empty words once more; yet in the end perhaps that's what those daily struggles were all about, as we fought for the right of a small group of people to live as human beings.

SECTION I

Travelling Tales

Chapter 1

Disillusioned

My original travel plans were vague. I knew so little about the reality of the country that I had no idea what I would find of special interest, and from previous journeys I had learnt that detailed itineraries are invariably abandoned due to unforeseen events. There was still a great deal of political uncertainty in Romania; the hastily elected National Salvation Front Government did not seem to be ringing the changes as fast as the population wanted and the press was full of reports of strikes and student marches. The possibility of a second revolution was even being mentioned, and I relished the prospect of witnessing it, perhaps being able to join forces with these brave people desperate to change their circumstances, risking all to chase their dreams.

I set aside nine months to tour the country. I imagined most of my time would be spent in the cities; from what I had read, the countryside in the south was full of nothing but flat ploughed fields and collective farms, and the mountainous regions of the north had been affected very little by what happened in the rest of the country, neither the strict Communist regime nor the ensuing revolution. It had not been viable to create collective farms in the mountains and the 'peasants' had been left with their small plots of land, living off subsistence farming as they had for centuries. Though I was sure they were fascinating and I certainly wanted to go there for a short while, they were not part of the great democratic movement I hoped to witness and did not feature greatly in my plans.

I prefer travelling on my own but I wimped out of doing so initially. Though I'd done my best with a colloquial Romanian book, the language was still beyond me and I didn't relish arriving alone in a large city with no one to turn to for help. So I arranged to spend the first six weeks with a journalist friend, David, who was writing about the anniversary of the revolution. I had travelled with him before and knew that we would probably make a good team, and he had some useful contacts amongst the foreign correspondents in Bucharest. I hoped the latter would fill in some of the many gaps in my knowledge and provide me with introductions to native Romanians. After those first six weeks David planned to leave and I would be on my own. I hoped that by then I would have picked up the language sufficiently and met enough local people to manage in Romanian alone.

My first impressions of Romania as we alighted from the plane on a cold December evening were pure George Orwell's *1984* – soldiers at the airport, guns everywhere, dim lighting, grim grey apartment blocks. The manager of the Hotel Parc accompanied us up in the lift, asking with a hopeful gleam in his eye whether we had come to Romania for a baby. I felt like kicking him but felt sufficiently intimidated by the guns at the airport to be ingratiating in my negative replies. We found a bug in our room, behind the bedside table, its wires still intact; its huge ostentation made it ridiculous, yet at the same time it was an intimidating reminder that Ceauşescu's world had been very real and that its legacy would remain for years. I screamed obscenities into it, just in case, and marvelled at there being hot water in the shower.

In the empty hotel restaurant we ate a surprisingly good

piece of beef, garnished to my astonishment with Chinese prawn crackers, and I fell for the waiter's story of saving up funds to go and study in the West. I was thrilled to have already found someone intent on changing his life in a way that would never have been possible a year ago, and I agreed to change dollars with him at what I knew to be well below the black market rate. A few days later I realized that this was a standard tale and most of Bucharest's waiters were working for the big black market dealers.

While my companion, David, pestered Government officials and tried to interview ministers, I spent my first few days as a simple tourist, wandering the streets of Bucharest just looking and smelling and listening. The buildings were a sad combination of old and new – sad because there was still enough left of the old city to imagine how magnificent it must have once been. Bucharest before the war was known as 'the Paris of the East', and it was easy to picture it – magnificent three-storey houses with ornate wooden porchways and turrets, outdoor balconies and steeply tiled roofs. Cramped between grey apartment blocks as though they had escaped the bulldozers only by mistake, they were mostly divided up into flats now like everything else.

Everywhere were reminders of the violence of the revolution. The beautiful 19th century National Library was riddled with bullet holes, as was the neighbouring Athenae Palace Hotel, hideout in the interwar years of spies and foreign correspondents. The police records' centre (funnily enough) had been gutted by fire, although the Government building next to it was strangely untouched. Outside the latter, a hideous Soviet-style modern art memorial had recently been unveiled as a tribute to those who had died in the revolution, but the soldiers on armed guard around it rather defeated the object, I thought.

I looked around for evidence of the new free market economy, but found little except kiosks selling Western cigarettes and Turkish whisky, and newspaper stands dominated by German porn magazines. The shops were poorly stocked, filled with nothing but pickled beans and endless dusty packets of prawn crackers – perhaps the unwanted product of some Communist deal with China years ago. In the centre of town there was a huge department store selling an extraordinary variety of useless items. It was impossible to find a pad of paper or a ball-point pen, yet I could have bought as many guitars, flower vases or canvas tents as I liked.

Most of the shoppers were outside in the cobbled streets queuing for bread and potatoes. I never saw any meat being sold throughout my stay in Bucharest, although there was always a plentiful supply in the state-run tourist restaurants and hotels where we ate in the evenings with the foreign correspondents. These places, though very cheap, were far beyond the means of ordinary people. I sat staring intently at the Romanians eating amongst us, longing to know what they had done to earn their wealth and become part of an élite. It was frustrating not knowing who were the baddies and who the heroes. Little did I know that I would soon have very real enemies of my own in this country, that I would come up against members of the old Communist regime and hate them in a way I never knew I was capable of. But for the moment it was just a sea of grey faces, no one looking very happy, keeping their faces down and their noses clean.

Foreign correspondents I found to be a strange breed. I'd expected impassioned young men straight out of *Fortunes of War*, full of enthusiasm and love for the country where they hoped to make their names. Instead I found them cynical and detached. They spoke only of the Government and its immediate plans; I found them useless at summing up the general feeling in the streets and the country as a whole. Through all their talk was filtered a strong dislike of the Romanian people. Most of them appeared strangely unmoved by the orphanage problem, and on the whole I felt uneasy in their company, guilty of admitting the romantic notions of what I had hoped to find in Romania.

I visited the famous House of the Republic, or 'Ceauşescu's Palace' as it has become known in the West. I had seen photos of it but was still unprepared for the sheer scale of the place. I felt physically sick as I looked at it, thinking of the money and effort put into a project so totally useless, while kids were dying in buildings little better than pigsties. Ceauşescu had bulldozed the oldest cathedral in Romania to make way for this great testament to Romania's success; apparently thousands had been evicted from their homes as the land was cleared. It was still not finished, and with rooms the size of football pitches, no one knew what to do with it. As I looked up at its thousands of broken windows I wished I could throw a bomb into it.

I took refuge in a smart-looking café in the wide modern boulevard that led up to the Palace, tempted by beautiful chocolate eclairs in the window. One bite though and I spat it out. It tasted foul, made of false chocolate and false cream. I wanted to be like Hunca Munca and go round smashing everything – this fake food and fake café and fake palace. It all felt like a not very well done film set; even the apartment blocks and the soldiers everywhere were too much of a cliché to seem real. No wonder Western propaganda had managed to paint such a grim picture of what had happened under Communism – because that's what it was, the reality of it, totally grim and devoid of human character.

I made a decision to stop looking for impressions and concentrate on the people. I wanted to meet Romanians as individuals, not as queues of grey people shivering against the cold. I pretended I was a reporter and began approaching passers-by, asking them for their views on life and the universe. A surprising number of people in Bucharest turned out to be relatively fluent in a foreign language, usually French but sometimes English. I soon found that queues were the best places for starting conversations. If I wandered down the back roads of Bucharest it was never long before I came across a long line of people, waiting to buy bread, potatoes, milk . . .

The bitter weather made people's physical appearance fairly uniform; everyone wore hats, either of sheepskin or of rabbit fur, and most were in thick woolly coats buttoned up over many layers of jumpers. Some of the men wore three-quarter length leather jackets in almost clichéd Communist style, with large lapels and thick waist straps. Fashion was evidently not a priority, even for the young – what mattered was keeping the cold out. As I bashed my boots together to stop my toes going numb I understood why, and I surprised even myself as I watched in envy, rather than my usual disdain, a woman walk past in a fur coat – it looked so *warm*.

As they waited, these people had hours to chatter about what they thought of the changes taking place in their country, and there was always a great deal of interest in a foreigner who wasn't in a diplomatic car or sitting in the Intercontinental Hotel. A crowd of people usually quickly gathered to tell me what they thought I needed to know; they obstinately refused, however, to tell me what I wanted to hear.

'Queues were never this long in Communist times,' an old man informed me, to a chorus of nodding heads from his neighbours.

'A loaf of bread used to cost just three *lei* – now it's ten!' (At the time there were about 200 Romanian *lei* to the pound.)

'I've been living off nothing but bread and potatoes for six months, we just can't afford anything else any more.'

'Iliescu's even worse than Ceauşescu. At least we didn't have this terrible inflation then.'

'But you can speak freely now,' I protested. 'A year ago you wouldn't even have been allowed to talk to me as you are now. You can read what you like, you can travel freely, you can visit the West. You can vote in elections, protest in street marches, start your own business, do the work that you want to do!'

'So bloody what? That doesn't make the price of a loaf of bread any less, does it? That doesn't stop my children telling me they're cold and hungry, does it? That doesn't make my heating work, does it?'

'Well no, but surely it must count for something?'

'What? What does it mean to the man in the street? Do you think any of us have enough money to travel to the West? Not that your Governments are letting us in anyway. It's next to impossible to get a visa, which is ironical considering how much Ceauşescu was criticized for not letting us travel.'

'And I can now do the work I want, can I? Have you seen the unemployment figures published yesterday? It's criminal! In the Communist years everyone had a job, you knew you weren't going to be suddenly made destitute with no way of providing for your family. We may not have been very rich, but at least we had work. My daughter is just finishing at university – well she would have been a great deal better off under the old system. In those days you were assigned a job straight after graduating and the country made the most of your skills. But now there's nothing for her, she'd been told there are no vacant positions for pharmacists. Next thing I know she'll be emigrating like all these other capable youngsters, and Germany and America will have stolen the best of Romania's workers.'

Slowly all my dreams, all my enthusiasm about these people that I'd been building up for months, came crashing down around me. 'NO!' I wanted to shout, 'you're not meant to be like this!'

'But what about freedom!' I wailed. 'What about democracy?'

'They're just empty words. If this is what your democracy means, then you can have it back.'

I tried to find out more about these people who were destroying my dreams, and I asked them what they did. A surprising number were professionals. In this particular crowd there were two teachers, an engineer, a chemist and a 'medical assistant', whatever that meant. Another was a taxi driver, while two others said they worked in local government. Almost all the women gave me a job description of some kind, which struck me as being very different from what I'd expect from a similar group of people at home. Two people in separate crowds pointed out to me vehemently that they were '*not* a peasant', that they were educated people. Many more stressed to me that they were *Christian* people.

'Ceauşescu wasn't such a bad man,' an old woman told me. 'In the early years he did so much for us. He turned us into a modern, industrialized nation. He built us all these apartment blocks, he gave us good jobs. And he put Romania on the map – he stood up against Russia, he was a brave man. All the other Eastern Bloc countries had Russian troops on their soil, but Ceauşescu wouldn't allow it. He was a good Romanian.'

I'd expected a certain amount of solidarity between the Eastern Bloc countries. Whenever I spoke of Poland, however, I was told that it was full of bloody Catholics, and I was constantly treated to the refrain, 'We are an island of civilized Latin people stuck in a barbaric Slavic sea.' A mere mention of Hungary would bring forth curses and spitting.

'They want Transylvania back. Well they can't have it, it's ours, we were there first. They treated us badly for centuries; now it's our turn to have the upper hand.'

'But it was a Hungarian priest in Timishoara who started the revolution,' I protested.

'Nonsense! It was the brave Romanian people who were slaughtered in their thousands.'

'All those boys killed in the revolution – it wasn't worth it. They died for a better life for the rest of us, but they died in vain. It was all a waste, nothing has improved.'

'Ceauşescu should never have been executed,' I was told. 'He didn't deserve that. He should have just been put in prison for a while.'

'Things were better with him; if he was alive I'd vote to have him back.'

I was almost speechless. 'But what about the way he destroyed people's lives?' I spluttered. 'People disappeared for doing or saying anything against him. What about the Securitate, the secret police?'

'At least they meant we didn't suffer from the terrible crime that we have now. Since the revolution it hasn't been safe to walk the streets at night.'

'But what about all his personal wealth,' I volunteered, 'while the rest of you were living in such poverty?'

'Well, we had more then than we did now, that's all I know. And anyway, he was our leader, of course he had to be wealthier than ordinary people, that's only right. Isn't your queen? And he spent much of the money on noble things – have you seen the House of the Republic? It's a wonderful testament to Romania's greatness.'

'And what about the orphanages, the thousands of children he locked up in virtual concentration camps?'

I received a huge variety of answers to the latter question, ranging from an embarrassed silence and claim of ignorance of the problem, to a total denial of its existence.

'They're fine now,' I was told. 'It was all grossly exaggerated.'

Many informed me that the orphanages were full of nothing but gypsy children, and therefore: 'It's not our problem. If the gypsies don't care for their kids, why should we have to foot the bill? It's not our fault, there's nothing we can do about it.'

'And anyway, it's not worth spending lot of money on

them, it wouldn't achieve anything. They're gypsies, they're born bad, it's in their blood. Nothing would turn them into good citizens, not all the money in the world.'

Others told me it was unfair that the West was highlighting the orphanages so much. It was only one of Romania's many problems; other people needed help too. On similar lines many thought it was simply stupid to give help to those who couldn't make use of it. If ordinary Romanians were given even a fraction of the amount being spent on these institutions, they would have the leg-up they needed to make Romania great again. But what could a handicapped child ever contribute to society? It was a waste. And anyway, every country treats its handicapped and unwanted children badly – it wasn't fair to single out Romania.

The gypsies were mentioned constantly as the main cause of Romania's current ills. They were thieves, I was told (as I looked around me I wondered what on earth they found to steal), and apparently they controlled the black market. Whenever I asked if anyone had thought of starting their own business, it was as if I'd said a very dirty word.

'I'm not a gypsy! I'm a civilized man of culture, I'm not involved with that.'

It seemed that 'business' – there is no Romanian word for it – was synonymous with corruption and bribery, and no one would admit to having anything to do with it. The gypsies were apparently getting extremely rich by practising it, but only at the expense of good honest Romanian citizens.

There was no notion of wealth creation; when I asked how they envisaged Romania's economy recovering, I was told repeatedly of their mineral reserves, their fertile agricultural land and vast grain fields. 'We are a rich country, we used to be known as the breadbasket of the East. As soon as Russia stops stealing our produce, we will have much to sell to the West.' I didn't have the heart to mention the vast European Community food surplus and the fact that none of the Western countries would want to buy their grain.

When I asked which party they would vote for at the next election, I was told time and time again: 'I hate politics, I am not political.' Despite a general belief that Iliescu, the President, was nothing but a Communist under another name, many held that the leaders of the two main opposition parties would be even more unsuitable as premiers. Campeanu, the head of the Liberals, had spent many years as a political prisoner before escaping to Paris where he established a pressure group informing the outside world of what was going on under Ceauşescu; Ion Ratsu, leader of the Peasants' Party, had emigrated to London and established a multi-million pound shipping business. What I had read of them sounded good; both had worked hard on behalf of political prisoners while in exile, they had established good contacts with Western leaders and they had first-hand experience of what life meant in a democracy. Both men's wives had set up charities to help the orphanages and seemed to be amongst the few people actually trying to deal with the problem from within Romania. I had thought they sounded much more suitable than Iliescu – a former crony of Ceauşescu's – for the task of leading Romania into democracy and a market based economy.

However, I was told that the crime of Campeanu and Ion Ratsu was in having gone abroad. They had not, it seemed, shared the Romanians' suffering through the bad times; instead they had been living it up in the West, and they had no right to come back now that things were easier, just to make even more money for themselves. Iliescu may not be much, I heard, but at least he'd always been here.

Another element was anti-Semitism. One of the criticisms against Petre Roman, the current prime minister, was the fact that his grandfather had been Jewish. This meant that he was most definitely not to be trusted and was bound to be working against Romania's national interests. I've always found such racism hard to deal with; if someone can hold such beliefs they are hardly going to be open to rational argument. I usually came out with a mere 'Don't be so ridiculous'.

'We know about Jews in Romania,' I was told. 'There used to be lots of them; they thought they were above us, they just used our labour and lived like kings off the money they made out of us. We don't want his type ruling this country.'

Even a doctor told me, when we were discussing the horrors of the war, that 'at least it got rid of the bloody Jews'. I was shocked to the core; I'd never seen such shameless anti-Semitism. The Holocaust suddenly became very real to me, as I began to understand the attitudes that had let it happen, and I found myself haunted by the way people spoke of the Jews – when I later travelled around the country, Jewish cemeteries were to become a minor obsession.

The issue of Romania's frontiers seemed to be far more important than what was going on inside the country itself. The same people who claimed to have no interest in politics would lecture me for hours on Romanian rights to Soviet Moldavia and the Hungarian question.

I learnt more about the latter from the foreign correspondents. Up until the end of the First World War, Transylvania had been part of Hungary and there are still about two and a half million Hungarians living there. They had been treated extremely badly by Ceauşescu and were now demanding more rights – they wanted their own Hungarian-speaking schools, their own Catholic churches, and the return of the houses and land that had been taken from them. The Romanians, however, were panicking that this was the thin end of the wedge, that next there would be demands for Transylvania to join Hungary again, for

Budapest still held a claim to it. The argument was based on the question of who was there first, and both sides had irrefutable evidence to prove that they were Transylvania's indigenous inhabitants. Apparently whoever won the dispute had the right to treat the losing side as abominably as they liked, since they should not have been there in the first place.

So much for my twenty million victims being cruelly suppressed by an evil tyrant. Where were the heroes? I felt angry that they weren't what I had wanted them to be, and also angry at myself that I could have been so wrong. I didn't understand, and I think that was the reason above all why I didn't simply return home there and then and find a more sympathetic people to write about. And anyway, Romanian Airways was on strike. I couldn't afford to fly on Swissair or Lufthansa, the only alternatives, so it seemed that I would have to stay for a while yet whether I liked it or not.

Through a contact of the British Council we arranged to spend Christmas with a priest and his family in Botiza, a small village in Maramuresh, held to be the most traditional and unspoilt area of Transylvania. It sounded romantic, and by now, fed up with the depressing atmosphere of the cities, I was dying to meet real 'peasants'. I pictured people resembling 19th century Russians serfs, hopelessly downtrodden and wretched. However, many townspeople told me of how rich the peasants had become since the revolution. 'They've been given all the land, you see, and they can sell their produce for whatever prices they like – that's why everything is so expensive now.' My image was further confused by the director of Cluj Ethnographic Museum informing me that the peasants not only owned foreign cars, but were now buying helicopters. 'I've seen it with my own eyes,' he said. When I mentioned that I hoped to see something of the old country traditions, he assured me that they had died out years ago. 'They all have colour televisions now,' he said.

Nevertheless, I was excited by the prospect of experiencing in a traditional village atmosphere Romania's first Christmas since the war. Much had been made of this in the international press; under Communism Romania had been atheist, Christmas was officially banned, and 25 December was listed in the calendar as just an ordinary working day. I imagined the priest as a long-suffering, learned old man, coming out of hiding and joyfully leading his flock out of the dark atheist years.

The overcrowded bus slid its way through the mountains from Baia Mare, and I became increasingly nervous as the driver took great swigs from his brandy bottle at every skid. After three hours we stepped off into deep snow. We'd been told we'd be met by the priest at the bus stop, and we looked round hopefully at the horses and carts. Everyone turned as a car approached; it wasn't one of the ubiquitous Dacias but a new Peugeot, and it stopped in front of us. A tall, darkly-bearded man in a thick dark coat emerged from the driver's side and I took a step backwards, feeling a little threatened. He addressed us in French, unsmiling, and asked if we were the English couple. When we nodded he swept us into the back of the Peugeot before leaping back behind the wheel and speeding off through the snow towards the mountains at the top of the valley.

We tried to make conversation but he simply gave gruff replies – it became clear that his French wasn't very good – and we ended up just staring out at the stunning snow-covered scenery.

Twenty minutes later we arrived at a village of dark timber houses lining a frozen stream. It was classically picturesque and old-fashioned. Small two- or three-roomed homesteads were fronted by ornate wooden gateways; cows peered over the doors of the barns adjoining almost every house, and smoke streamed steadily from every chimney. The timber made everything seem Bavarian, and as we spotted Botiza's villagers I truly felt as though I had stepped back in time. There were men dressed in cream woollen jackets, embroidered ornately at collar and cuff. Below their woollen leggings they wore extraordinary boat-shaped pieces of leather – I later discovered it to be pigskin – in place of shoes, strapped on to their legs with leather thongs. They wore black sheepskin hats, and their faces were red from the cold. All were busy – leading horses, chopping wood, loading hay. At the river, women in brightly-coloured patterned headscarves were breaking through the ice and collecting water in enamel buckets. They looked up as we passed, and appeared to be commenting to each other on the priest's new guests.

As we rounded the corner in the middle of the village I looked ahead and the spell was broken. A large concrete church loomed before us, and as we pulled up beside a big modern two-storey stone house, I had a terrible feeling of impending doom.

We followed the priest up the stone steps and walked through a large hall to a carpeted sitting room. There we met the priest's wife and three teenage daughters, dressed in jeans and listening to pop music on a Japanese cassette recorder. They gave us short frosty 'hellos' and showed us to a room with one small double bed. I felt embarrassed, for I had thought that they knew we weren't a couple, but we kept quiet and unpacked, unsure why we felt such unwelcome intruders.

A little later, we all sat down for a formal meal of bland tinned foods and similar conversation. The family had visited Western Europe and told us they had particularly liked France, listing all the wonderful clothes they had bought there as well as the car. They asked us nothing about ourselves or our impressions of Romania, just told us how marvellous life was for 'the people' now that they could worship freely. 'Christianity reigns once more,' toasted the priest, and I lamely raised my glass.

After the meal our host offered to show me round his church. It was huge, far bigger than a usual parish church at home, and apparently had been built eight years previously by master builders sent up especially from Bucharest. There were beautiful gold leaf murals covering the inside walls and thick carpets on the floor. As I looked around me I suddenly burst into tears. I kept picturing rows of wailing orphans rotting in filth and I wanted to scream. This was all so rich, so disgustingly lavish, and it felt almost evil.

I was confused. If this had been built eight years ago, that was at the height of the Communist years. So what was all that about the poor old Church being persecuted by the evil atheist Ceauşescu? All that rubbish about believers coming out of hiding and celebrating their first Christmas since the war? My dreams of an idyllic Yuletide were shattered; but it was more than that. I had always thought of Christianity being such a powerful force of goodness and truth in Eastern Europe. To suddenly face the reality that the Church had done very well out of the old regime shocked me to the core, and the part of me that believes passionately in God felt threatened. I felt an overwhelming need to escape.

Tears streamed down my face and the priest stood beside me looking most concerned. I mumbled something about never having been away from Christmas before and feeling homesick, before bolting out into the snow. I flew straight into David, about to join me on my church tour. I sank my head into his shoulder and sobbed, pleading with him to think of a way we could leave this place and go anywhere else for Christmas the next day.

David was very calm and practical, telling me to try to be professional, to imagine that I was a journalist and to think of what amazing articles we'd be able to write about the corruption of the Church and the role of state-paid priests in a Communist regime. We had no way of leaving anyway, we were stuck here till Boxing Day at the earliest, so we'd have to make the best of it. He suggested a walk in the village and tried to cheer me up as we slid down the frozen track, launching forth with raucous Christmas carols and every religious joke he could think of.

As we wandered our way up the track we stepped back to a Europe of two hundred years ago. Villagers, dressed in their strange, beautiful clothes, nodded at us warily. The houses were higgledy-piggledy, often with sinking foundations and hazardly tilting roofs. Next to the houses were barns, many of which were far larger than the houses. Animal noises dominated the atmosphere as horses pawed at the snow and snorted out steamy breath to clear their nostrils of tiny icicles. We found an old wooden water-mill built over one of the smaller streams which fed the larger river we had followed up the valley. Seeing us taking pictures, an old man came out from the doorway and waved us across the log bridge to see the workings of the mill more closely. The large wheel was simultaneously grinding maize and powering a saw that was cutting logs. I sat down and listened to the rhythm of the sawing, feeling calmer. The priest may not have been what I expected, but here were people I felt I could love.

We went further up the village, slipping over regularly on the icy pathways. Darkness fell and people began to disappear inside their houses. We were reluctantly deciding to head back to the priest's when a little old woman dressed in black rushed up to us; as she pulled at our arms we realized she was insisting that we come into her house to get warm. We followed her over a tiny bridge, through a carved gateway and climbed up wooden steps, walking through a simple doorway straight into a small, brightly-painted room. It was dominated by a solid fuel stove, over which she immediately busied herself with a water and herb concoction that she insisted was tea. I looked around the room. The walls were painted light blue, and covered in ornate stencilled patterns of flowers and leaves. On each wall were religious pictures, crucifixes, and beautifully embroidered pieces of material hung up as decoration. Behind the stove, up against the far wall, was a bed, covered in a thick rug and large lumpy cushions. By the window opposite the stove was a small wooden table and two stools, one of which I was invited to sit on. Home-made rugs, made of what seemed to be strips of scrap material woven together, covered the wooden floor.

The old woman suddenly took my hand and led me into the adjoining room; together these two rooms made up the house. This room contained one more bed and another table. None of the other houses we'd seen had been any bigger than this. It was a family's home I realized, as I was shown the framed pictures kept in this 'best room' of her late husband and three sons. I thought of them all squashed in here with barely room to move.

We communicated mainly through sign language. Her name was Aneka, and in fact she was much younger than she looked – only sixty-three, when I'd imagined her to be at least eighty. Her youngest son, Theodor, came in and cheerily shook hands. He peeled off two layers of jerseys and warmed his hands by the fire before pouring us tumblerfuls of stuff that he called *tsuica*, a clear spirit made from plums which we were expected to down in one. I sat in the chair while David and Theodor seated themselves on the bed by the fire. We clinked glasses and wished each other '*la mults ann*', a long life, while Aneka, refusing a drink, pottered about the stove preparing food for her son.

Seemingly word of our presence had quickly spread and the small room soon began filling up with interested neighbours, all very friendly and bearing bottles of alcohol. Many of the men, including Theodor, told us that they worked in a gold mine farther up the valley. They bombarded us with questions about the price of gold in the West, and about the wages of miners back in Britain – to the latter they sat back and shook their heads in wonder (they were earning about 15 US dollars a month). Others amongst them worked in forestry, while some were craftsmen – there was a roofer and a farrier. The women all seemed to be in charge of the homesteads – everyone owned pigs, cows and often horses.

Two hours later, by now very drunk but a great deal happier, we set off in a large group and carol-sung our way around the village. David and I picked up the words to the choruses of the main carols, and our participation resulted in great slaps on the back. A few times we gave them a not very tuneful rendering of 'Oh Come All Ye Faithful', and at last I began to feel truly in the Christmas spirit. Every household we screeched to invited us in for yet more *tsuica* and pieces of Christmas walnut cake, apart from the priest's house where we were each solemnly handed a single walnut out on the doorstep. It went on and on till almost six in the morning, by which time I was so drunk I couldn't stand unsupported.

The revelry continued for three days and we spent as much time as we could away from the priest's house. On the day after Christmas, pigs were slaughtered and we were encouraged to eat as much as we could of the chunks of meat roasted on open fires. Street pantomimes toured the village; according to the priest they were nativity plays but there seemed to be far more people dressed up as bears and devils than shepherds or wise men. There would always be a man acting as 'the wicked Jew', who at the end of the performance was always hanged and set fire to at the bus stop. Ploughs dug through the ice of the roads, apparently symbolizing the imminence of spring. The mishmash of different beliefs and superstitions was fascinating, sometimes frightening; always I had that same feeling of having stepped back in time to a world that had long since disappeared in Western Europe.

Before New Year we travelled to Bukovina, an area in northern Moldavia famed for its painted monasteries. In the town of Gura Humorlui we met some young people – students and young teachers who could speak a little English – who invited us to join their New Year party. We gladly accepted, but grew increasingly depressed as the evening wore on. The general atmosphere was of great gloom. Our companions spoke of nothing but how terrible everything was since the revolution – of how jobs were no longer secure, of how prices had gone up, of how young people were no longer being given apartments. David and I ended up building a snowman outside and toasting in 1991 alone, since no one else could think of anything to look forward to.

I made up my mind to go home for my animals. My previous travels had been with a donkey and two dogs across the hills of Spain, France and Italy. I'd kept away from large towns, made absolutely no great discoveries of use to other travellers, and I'd had the time of my life. This time I had wanted to be a more serious traveller; I'd wanted to make a contribution to the understanding of the changes taking place in Romania. But it seemed that there weren't really any great changes, and to understand why, I reckoned there would be no better way than travelling back in time to see the kind of people who'd inhabited Romania before the Communist takeover. Pre-war Romania had had an 80 per cent peasant population; if I travelled in a suitably traditional way amongst those who had survived intact, I thought, I'd have the best chance to learn about the true national character.

I returned to Bosnia and planned to start my donkey travels from there. As a gesture of solidarity to the much maligned gypsies I found a craftsman to make me a small wooden caravan; in fact it turned out resembling a miniature Wild West wagon, with hoops and a canvas top. I promised Aneka, who was beginning to treat me as a daughter, despite my still not being able to say a full sentence to her, that I'd be back before Easter, and I flew back to Britain to fetch my proposed mode of transport – my faithful donkey, Hannibal, and my two canine protectors – Georgie, my beautiful little Battersea mongrel, and William, my great big soppy Dobermann.

Chapter 2

Tales of Tyrants

I went home to organize my new plans and found my mother so pleased at the prospect of being relieved of the care of my animals that she agreed to lend me her Land Rover to drive them out in. I had already decided to make my home in France at the end of my Romanian travels, so the decision to take the dogs out of England for good had already been made and it was just a question of when. But it was still a frightening moment driving on to the cross-channel ferry with them, the point of no return. Hannibal the donkey was towed in a trailer behind. With all the horses in Romania I was probably mad to take him all the way across Europe, but I had grown inordinately fond of him during our first journey together and I knew how much he'd love to be on the road again. He's a Poitou, a pedigree donkey of vast size and strength. He had never fallen ill on me, he would eat anything he could lay his jaws upon, and I knew I wouldn't have any problems with him, so even though I was carting coals to Newcastle I reckoned madder things had been done in the name of love.

I arranged to lend the Land Rover for the duration of my donkey travels to a volunteer group from Scotland working at an orphanage called Yonashen in northern Moldavia. A journalist who had written about them recommended I help them, for they were apparently in dire need of a decent vehicle. Though somewhat chaotic and amateurish, she said they had apparently achieved miraculous change at what had been one of the worst institutions found after the revolution.

The project had been started the previous summer by a young unemployed skateboard champion with the extraordinary name of Moona Wolfe Murray. In June he had accompanied a friend driving an aid truck out to Romania; they had dropped supplies at Yonashen and Moona had been so horrified by what they saw there that he decided to stay. A great deal of aid had previously been given to Yonashen but there was no evidence of it; it had all been stolen by corrupt management and staff. A hundred and twenty children were being controlled by just four peasant women, who resorted to canes to keep their charges locked up within the walls of a decrepit old building.

Moona, now joined by his brother Rupert, a journalist who quickly organized a charity base in Edinburgh and began fund-raising projects, had gradually built up a volunteer presence at Yonashen which ensured that the donated supplies actually reached the children. I was fascinated to see what they were doing and arranged to spend June with them, hoping I'd be able to give them some publicity and thereby help them raise funds, and maybe, I thought, I'd be able to make a small contribution whilst I was there.

So, my plan was to drive out to Botiza, swap the Land Rover for the donkey cart and travel eastwards through Transylvania, across the Carpathians towards the north-eastern corner of Moldavia. There I would stop at Yonashen, the orphanage, for about a month, before resuming my travels and heading south towards the Hungarian areas of central Romania. I aimed to be back home in September, reckoning that six months was plenty of time to cover the relatively small distances involved.

My research into Romania changed tack. I was aware

that I'd begun with entirely the wrong attitude – because they were white and European I'd expected Romanians to behave as I hoped I would had I lived through forty years of a Communist dictatorship. But it was more complicated than that. Forty years ago Romania had been nothing like Britain. I began devouring books on Romanian history as though I were trying to solve a crime, and I was soon fascinated.

The history of Romania makes that of Britain seem very boring. It is dominated by tales of bloodthirsty tyrants and great patriotic leaders – of Vlad the Impaler and Elizabeth the Blood Countess, of Stephen the Great and Michael the Brave. Stuck between the East and the West, Romania has never been left alone by its neighbours – its rich gold and mineral deposits and fertile southern plains made it a prize worth fighting for. When the Romans colonized the country they found enough gold to enable them to stop all taxes for two years – Romania was able to fund their entire military operations throughout the empire.

The Romans left their language and a dark-haired population which somehow managed to survive the Dark Ages more or less intact. They were continually overrun by barbarians and Slavic hordes, and to escape from the invaders some of them moved north from the southern Danubian plains and into the mountainous area now known as Transylvania. At about the same time – the exact date is the source of the dispute over territorial rights – the Szeckler settlers came from Hungary. Soon they were joined by Germans from Saxony who established themselves in the seven walled towns of Transylvania known as the 'Siebensburgen'.

Throughout most of the Middle Ages, Transylvania was part of the Austro-Hungarian Empire. The Hungarians and the Saxons shared power and enjoyed relative autonomy, whilst the Romanians in their midst – over half the population – were treated little better than slaves. They were not allowed to worship their orthodox faith, they were not allowed to own land, and in the Siebensburgen they were not even allowed to walk the streets with shoes on. Meanwhile the two other Romanian provinces – Wallachia in the south and Moldavia in the east – from the 15th century onwards were constantly invaded by the Turks. Moldavia was ruled by Turkish princes almost continually until the 19th century, when Russian 'protection' replaced them. Wallachia tried to keep its independence by playing off its two dominant neighbours, Turkey and Austria-Hungary, against each other. The great heroes of Romanian history are those who had the courage and cunning to stand up against these imperial enemies; the cost of their ventures in terms of loss of life and the fact that their gains never lasted more than a few years did not diminish their glorification as patriotic heroes.

Thus Vlad the Impaler is an enormously admired figure in Romanian history and in many ways he typifies the endless struggle to establish Romanian independence. He is the evil character on whom the Dracula myth is based; his murderous exploits struck terror throughout the Western world, for they coincided with the invention of the printing press and his Saxon victims tried to gain support by publicizing their plight. He was known as Dracula to friend and foe alike, even signing his name as such, apparently delighting in the impression it gave – in Romanian, Dracula means 'son of the devil'.

As Prince of Wallachia, Vlad went on raids into neighbouring Transylvania, murdering Germans and Hungarians as if for fun. His speciality was impaling, for which he devised an elaborate etiquette. Commoners would be randomly hurled over sharpened stakes, while knights and noblemen would have to suffer extra touches of sadism. One of Vlad's favourites was the rounded stake, upon which the victim was sat while ropes were fastened to each ankle; the other ends were tied to horses, who were then galloped away in opposite directions.

Vlad escaped Hungarian wrath by aligning himself to the Turkish emperor, paying him taxes in return for protection. In mid-career, however, he changed tactics and secured Hungarian backing by going to battle against the Turks instead. There is a story popular amongst Romanians of how the Turkish emperor turned back his entire army when he came across the remains of the advance party he had sent to negotiate with Vlad – the road was lined for miles with their dismembered carcasses up on stakes. The stench of rotting flesh is said to have sapped all courage from the Turks, who were legendary as the most bloodthirsty of fighters. They got Vlad in the end, of course, but for many years he made sure that Romania was never a permanent jewel in the Sultan's crown – and for that his people loved him.

Elizabeth Barthory was a member of the Hungarian nobility who ruled Transylvania in the 16th century. Like her fellow countrymen, she was hard on her Romanian servants, and one day, whilst beating her young maid, some of the girl's blood fell on her hand. Barthory was convinced that her skin had been softened and made beautiful by the virgin's blood and thought that she had found the secret of eternal youth. Thus began the systematic torture and murder of what is reckoned to be over seven hundred young girls. The blood bath became Elizabeth's speciality; she had an iron cage lined with spikes into which she would put the naked girls, and with red hot pokers she would force them to impale themselves on the sides of the cage. Beneath it was a bath to collect the blood, in which Elizabeth would bathe whilst it was still warm.

The Blood Countess was only stopped when she became over-ambitious and chose girls of the Hungarian nobility rather than Romanian peasants as her victims. She spent the rest of her life locked away in her castle; as a member of Transylvania's ruling family it was not considered right to execute her.

As the Ottoman Empire weakened in the 19th century, Moldavia and Wallachia were periodically occupied by both the Austrians and the Russians. They finally achieved full independence in 1877, when they united and adopted the name 'Romania'. The Romanian peasants in Transylvania made repeated attempts to overthrow their Hungarian landlords, but they had little hope of success against the might of the powerful Austro-Hungarian empire. Hungarian remained the official language of schools and public life; Catholicism remained the official religion. 'Greater Romania', including Transylvania, only came about after Austria-Hungary's defeat in the First World War. The social structure remained feudal, headed by a Hohenzollern royal family donated by Germany in 1866.

At the end of the 19th century came a Golden Age when Bucharest was named 'the Paris of the East' and the Romanian intelligentsia flourished; trade, however, continued to be dominated by foreigners – by the Germans and Hungarians of Transylvania and increasingly, especially in northern Moldavia, by the Jews who came to escape from the Russian pogroms. A capitalist middle class never developed amongst the Romanians themselves; there was no industrial revolution and no gradual introduction of democracy or modern political ideas.

Universal suffrage came suddenly after 1919, but the traditional liberal parties had no experience or clout to stand up against the extreme politics of the period and a king determined to establish a royal dictatorship. The popular Peasants' Party grew increasingly fascist, with a military wing known as the Iron Guard; anti-Semitic laws mirrored those being enacted in Germany and a strong secret police ruthlessly rounded up Communist activists influenced by the Russian revolution. I thought of all those articles I'd read about how Eastern Europe must go back to how it was before Communism and start again, and I groaned. The reality of the inter-war years was as ugly as the Communist era.

The Second World War was a disastrous time for Romania. It joined Hitler's invasion of Russia, annexing a large chunk of Soviet territory but suffering heavy losses under bombing from the British and Americans. In 1944 Romania changed sides, as the Germans and the Red Army fought over it, and in 1945 at Yalta, almost half of Moldavia was awarded to the Russians.

And then came the Cold War years. Yalta gave Stalin the influence he wanted and Kremlin-backed Communists rapidly took control of the post-war Government, aided by the permanent threat of complete Russian invasion. King Michael was forced to abdicate in 1947; land reforms followed which took property not only from the gentry but also robbed the peasants of their smallholdings. Russian troops remained on Romanian soil until 1958. Only the mountainous areas in the north were safe, where the land was not suitable for the mechanization of collective farms. Rapid industrialization took place as the Communist leaders determined to modernize Romania overnight.

Nicolae Ceauşescu was the uneducated son of a shoemaker from Wallachia, who in the pre-war fascist years had spent a great deal of time in political prisons. During the 1950s and 1960s he quietly worked his way to the top of the socialist hierarchy, until in 1967 he became President. His domestic policy grew increasingly Stalinist, reinforcing the powers of the secret police, ruthlessly disposing of any opponents, and indoctrinating the population with his cult of the personality. At the same time he took a surprisingly independent line on foreign policy, refusing to support Russia in international affairs and thus earning most favoured status from many Western countries. Britain even gave Ceauşescu a knighthood, and David Steel presented him with a Labrador puppy.

My reading wandered from Romanian history for a while as I looked into what had happened in the rest of the Eastern Bloc. The post-war history of East Germany, Poland, Hungary and Czechoslovakia is dominated by the names of brave men – Alexander Dubcek, Imre Nagy, Lech Walesa – who attempted to stand up against the Communist yoke in a way that never happened in Romania. They had supported Russia on an international level in the hope that in return they would be allowed to soften up on social and economic issues at home. Romania, however, seemed to have done the opposite, defying Moscow over many international issues but happily following a rigidly Stalinist domestic policy.

I slowly began to understand the secret of Ceauşescu's success. He effectively played on the historical insecurities of a nation plagued by an understandable inferiority complex. He was a strong leader who dared to stand up to a much more powerful imperial neighbour. Most of the population had never known the personal and economic freedom that Westerners had taken for granted for centuries; national pride and independence probably came much higher in their list of priorities. As the Romanians saw it, if no one was very rich, at least they no longer had to suffer the humiliation of seeing the Hungarians, Germans and Jews in their midst doing so much better than they were. The Communists' crimes against humanity and freedom were no worse than what had gone on for centuries before. It took the economic deprivations of the late 1980s, together with *glasnost*'s lessening of the threat from Russia, to convince most Romanians that totalitarian rule was too high a price to pay for the security of their borders.

Chapter 3

My Ass and I

From a travel writer's point of view, my travels with a donkey and cart around Romania were a disaster. As I set off through the mountains of Maramuresh I met with nothing but kindness and generosity; I received nothing but offers of food and shelter, and was welcomed into simple peasants' homes in every village we passed through. For week after week absolutely nothing went wrong – no disasters, no great tests of my courage and bravery, and the fear that had been my constant companion throughout my travels in Western Europe vanished completely. Even at the time it seemed too good to be true.

I found the dream of that right wing band of British politicians who hanker after Victorian values and traditional families. I went back to a world without cars or televisions, without divorce, without rock 'n' roll, and in it I found a degree of friendliness I hadn't known was possible. I learnt how to spin wool on a wooden spinning wheel, how to weave it into cloth and how to embroider the shirts and jackets of traditional Romanian national dress. I sheared sheep by hand, I scythed hay, I learnt how to cut a pig's throat and smoke its fat. I distilled my own brandy and, with enough of it inside me, even mastered Romanian folk dancing.

My greatest problem, in fact, was coping with the food. The staple diet of the peasants of Transylvania is *slanina* –

smoked pork fat, accompanied by a yellow gunge known as *mamaliga* made from coarsely ground maize meal and water. The fat – which doesn't contain even a hint of meat and is usually still attached to the skin and hairs – is laid out in thick slabs on one side of the plate, a great dollop of *mamaliga* is put on the other, and that's it – no pickles or chutneys, no vegetables, in fact nothing at all to help wash it down and mask the taste. My tonsils were the trouble. Once my tongue had identified the chunks of fat, they would go into revolt and gag at any attempts to swallow. I would usually be seated at a table surrounded by an entire family, spurring me on with tales of what a healthy pig my mouthful had once been a part of, reared lovingly by them since birth. They would not be eating – not for Romanians was there the prolonged social ritual of Mediterranean mealtimes. They almost always ate separately, the children as soon as the food was cooked, the father when he came in from work, and the mother ate the leftovers whenever she had time. A guest was certainly not to be insulted by her hosts eating alongside her. Instead they would just watch, ready to fetch more for me and make sure all my needs were catered for.

I am not a skinny person, and there seemed something ludicrous about someone of my dimensions forcing myself to eat platefuls of pure fat. The possibility of refusal, however, was rarely available. Often it was all that they had in the house, and protestations of not being hungry were never believed. If I turned up my nose at their offerings I was insulting both their generosity and their husbandry skills, for they instantly presumed that I thought their food was bad and would make me ill. Claims of being vegetarian were of little use either, since very few of them had ever heard of vegetarianism. If I tried to explain, they always thought it was the most ridiculous nonsense and became even more adamant that I should eat up their *slanina* since I must be in especially dire need of nourishment.

I did, however, find a solution of sorts. *Tsuica*, the spirit made from plums, was always served with the meal, be it breakfast or a teatime snack. I discovered that if I swigged this back once I had the food in my mouth, I could fool my tonsils and successfully swallow. Requests for more *tsuica* were taken as a great compliment to the family's skills in distillation and I was usually given enough to get me through the whole plateful. Consequently I have never been so drunk as when wandering around northern Romania. I was often to be seen as early as seven o'clock in the morning lying sprawled in my cart yelling newly-learned folk songs to the world, hiccuping uncontrollably and remarking on the beauty of my donkey as he wound his own way through the mountains or grazed contentedly from a ditch at the side of the road. Luckily, getting riotously drunk is something of a national pastime in Romania so this was not considered particularly out of the ordinary.

A few weeks into my trip I discovered the greatest contribution of Eastern Europe to international cuisine – 'gogosh', known to the Western world as doughnuts. In most households they were only made occasionally as treats for children, and I confess to having uttered a few little white lies to encourage spur of the moment *gogosh* making sessions that would not otherwise have taken place. A frequent line of questioning concerned the differences between Britain and Romania and what I liked here that did not exist at home. I managed to squeeze doughnuts into this category, claiming that we had nothing even resembling them back in Britain. Most women took a great deal of pride in their *gogosh* making skills, so this would usually bring forth a promise that *their* doughnuts were infinitely superior to any that I may have tasted elsewhere in Romania. Out would come the fat pan, yeast would be begged from a neighbour, and my saliva glands would start working overtime at the thought of what was to come.

Gogosh must be eaten straight from the pan while still

piping hot. Children and visiting Westerners gather round the stove waiting to grab the golden rounds from the bowl of sugar where they are placed by the chef. You have to eat very quickly or you miss out on your turn for the next batch, and it is considered bad form to give up before the whole lot have been finished. My record was thirteen, egged on by a little boy of eight who managed fourteen, and I couldn't do up the button on my jeans for three days afterwards.

Thus I made my way eastwards, living off little but brandy and doughnuts. I began my journey in March, when most of the snow had melted from the mountains around Botiza, although spring came slowly and it was still often bitterly cold. The Maramuresh area is bleak compared with the eastern side of the Carpathians and the wind would sweep fiercely across the bare hills. The greatest physical hazard to my travels in those first weeks, however, was often mud. The melting snows left a quagmire of slush in the valleys, and the dirt roads and tracks turned from the lethal ice rinks they had been at Christmas into almost impenetrable barriers of deep slop. The Romanians had a wonderful word for it – '*glod*' – that seemed to sum up the way the mud got into and on to everything. Hannibal's coat was thick with it, the cart was covered in it, my boots were always caked in it. The thought of tarmac and concrete pavements could make me dizzy with longing.

My progress was exceptionally slow, due mainly to the fact the villages are built in linear fashion, stretching for miles along the dirt roads and often merging into each other. It was very hard to pass a house without being stopped with enquiries as to who I was, where I was going and why, and consequential offers of sustenance and lodging. Often choosing where to stay would become a matter of great difficulty requiring all my reserves of tact and discretion, for I'd be surrounded by anything up to twenty people listing the advantages of staying at their particular abode.

'I've got plenty of maize for your donkey.'

'I've got wheat!'

'My hay comes from the best part of the valley, I'll give you some to take with you when you leave tomorrow!'

'My children are staying with their grandparents, you can have a bed to yourself.' (This one was a winner, since usually I had to share.)

Hannibal had never been as well fed in his life – I even had to widen the shafts of the cart because they started rubbing on his belly – breaking all the rules about giving donkeys nothing but grass or hay as he feasted nightly on great bucketfuls of maize. The cows and pigs in the barn behind the house would be squeezed together to make room for him, and I would often have great difficulty in persuading him to come out in the morning. I found that Hannibal's appearance impressed most Romanians enormously. The only donkeys they'd ever seen were tiny short-haired animals, so Hannibal's size and thick coat were marvelled at.

'If the donkeys in the West are like that, just imagine what the horses must be like!' I once heard a man remark to his neighbour, and I contemplated coming back with a carthorse.

My method of travel though was not generally approved of. Few could see why on earth anyone would choose to live like a gypsy, especially when they discovered that I had actually entered the country by car and dumped it. This was total madness, and I would be questioned for hours about what kind of car it was, its age, how fast it went and how much it was worth. The latter resulted in yet more lying, since if I admitted that I had a car worth £2,000 it meant that I must be *extremely* rich and triggered off endless requests for donations, so I usually kept the price at about a tenth of that, as I wondered whether it had been written off yet by a crazy Scottish aid worker. Another very popular question that flummoxes me to this day concerned the border post through which I had entered Romania. This was terribly important and interesting, often far more so than which country I had come from in the first place.

People's knowledge of world geography was peculiar. My saying that I came from England produced noddings of the head – they'd all heard of it and a large number knew of Churchill, who apparently was a very bad man, and Margaret Thatcher, who was truly wonderful. But very few actually knew where England was. There was a great deal of astonishment at my assertion that Britain was an island, especially from the ones who knew that it was in Europe. Many thought Britain was part of America, but my favourite came from a man who thought I was from the Middle East.

'Ah, England!' he said. 'That's next to Iraq, isn't it?'

'No, it's a long, long way from Iraq.'

'But you've just been at war with Iraq, so you must share a border with it.'

My attempt to explain the origins of the Gulf War only resulted in his conclusion that Kuwait must be part of Britain's empire, whereupon I gave up.

I also found that the pound sterling was unheard of by most. They all knew about dollars, and many thought that was simply the universal currency of the West. When I tried to explain the different currencies of Europe, most somehow jumped to the conclusion that Britain must be by far the wealthiest country in the world, since the pound was worth more than anything else. Germany couldn't possibly be richer if it took three Deutschmarks to buy a single pound. As for Italy, their economy must be worse than even Romania's.

I managed to pick up the language surprisingly quickly this time, due mainly to the fact that I was on my own, so unless I wanted to converse with no one but my animals for the next five months, I had to. But it was also because I've never met people who talk quite so much. Even before I understood little more than '*buna ziua*' (hello) and '*multsumesc*' (thank you), they would chatter to me constantly, as I sat and hoped my nods of agreement were coming at vaguely the right moments. Most of them had never met a foreigner before and it was as if they couldn't conceive of someone *not* understanding them. As ever, children were far and away the best teachers. While their parents were nattering away in long convoluted sentences, I would point to various objects in the room and look questioningly at the children, who would giggle and tell me its Romanian name slowly and clearly, astonished but rather pleased by my stupidity. Within about three weeks I was fluent enough to get by well enough on the main topics of conversation – animals and farming techniques, the relative wages of Britons and Romanians, family relationships and the institution of the monarchy.

Most of the Romanians I met whilst travelling in the mountains passionately wanted a restitution of the old royal family. They spoke misty eyed of Queen Marie, the Scottish granddaughter of Queen Victoria who had married King Carol and become a popular if highly individual First Lady. She was famous for riding the streets of Bucharest dressed in traditional Romanian dress, and for restoring a chain of old castles and turning them into beautifully furnished summer holiday homes. Her autobiography had recently been republished after years of being banned during the Communist era and it was charging to the top of the Romanian bestseller lists. In the cities I had found much more republican feeling, based mainly on dislike of the monarchy's foreign German origins. But from what I heard, this branch of the Hohenzollerns had taken Romania to heart, changing to Orthodox religion and passionately fighting for the dream of 'Greater Romania'. The last King's sister, exiled to the United States, had taken with her a sack of earth which she placed under her bed at the birth of each of her children so that each could be born on Romanian soil.

Reasons for wanting the King back were usually based on the certainty that he would be able to cure all the country's problems. There would never be such high inflation if the King were in charge and he would instantly solve all the recent unemployment by hiring everyone currently out of work, since he would obviously need lots of servants and a big army. I got nowhere in my attempts to suggest that if the government *did* decide to allow him back, King Michael would not be given the power or the money to do any of these things. They argued that Britain had a Queen and Britain was a rich country, wasn't it? When I let on that we had over three million unemployed, it could only mean that our Queen wasn't a very nice one.

Although I was never actually accused of lying, I learnt to recognize a certain expression that came to their faces whenever I was speaking such obvious nonsense as life being hard for some in the West. They refused to believe that it could be anything but total paradise full of Coca-Cola and Hula-Hoops. (It completely flummoxed me how so many of them knew about the latter – and they meant the potato snacks, not the playground game as I originally presumed – until I discovered that Ceauşescu had used Hula-Hoops as an example of the extreme corruption of Western Europe. The totally unnecessary conversion of a potato into hollow finger-shaped rings showed to what extent the working classes were being manipulated by the capitalist market. Consequently Romanians thought they sounded marvellous and often asked me if I could send them some when I returned home.) It was a constant uphill struggle trying to convince them that everyone was not stinking rich. Almost all of them had seen *Dallas*, so they *knew* what it was really like.

In most larger villages someone had a television, usually the priest. At seven o'clock on a Sunday evening the unfortunate owner's living room would be crammed full of as many neighbours as could fit in, armed with snacks of hard-boiled eggs and slivers of pork skin, ready for their weekly entertainment. As soon as the titles came up the audience would burst into riotous song:

'Di-daah, di-daah,
Di-dah di-di dah-dah,
Daah-daah-daah, da-da-daah!'

Names were shouted out in triumph as the viewers recognized the characters appearing on the screen.

'Bobby!'
'Pim!'
'Jar!'

Since it was subtitled, the noise level remained high throughout the programme, but I was usually given pride of place next to the screen since I understood the language. (This fact often increased confusion over Britain's whereabouts. If we spoke the same tongue, Britain *must* be very near America.) Few could read the tiny print of the subtitles and I was frequently asked to translate, especially when any sum of money was mentioned in which case I was expected immediately to give the equivalent in Romanian *lei*, to thrilled gasps from all. The favourite parts of the programme, however, were always those involving J.R.'s affairs, especially when they involved activity in swimming pools or elevators, and Sue Ellen's descent into alcoholism was also particularly hilarious.

Although I often cursed the impression of the West that it gave, I found myself enjoying these Sunday evenings immensely and the claim to possession of a television was a sure way of securing my stay in a particular house if it was made on a Sunday. The episodes of *Dallas* being shown were amongst the first, made in the late 1970s, and they only added to a feeling of somehow having stepped back in time.

As I made my way from Maramuresh into Transylvania this feeling was reinforced by my introduction to a breed of animal that seemed far more suited to a Gandhi film than a part of Europe that had to endure Siberian winters – buffalo. They were owned generally by people who could not afford both a cow and a horse, since buffaloes do the lot: pull the cart, plough the fields, and provide both meat and milk. I soon determined to take a pair home with me when I left, such wonderful animals did they seem. Their milk is the most delicious stuff I have ever tasted, thick and rich without being too creamy, whiter than cows' milk and without the strong tang of goats' or sheep's milk. Apparently it has the highest protein content of any milk and makes the most scrumptious ice cream, although a universal lack of freezers in the area prevented me from testing out the latter claim. Another feature I particularly liked was the way buffaloes' front hooves were shod. They wore exquisitely-made little moon-shaped iron shoes, enabling them to walk great distances without going lame. Cows and oxen sometimes wore these, too, and I have endless photographs of different types of bovine footwear being held up by utterly perplexed owners, astonished by this foreign girl shrieking with delight at the sight of their animals.

Taking lifelike photographs proved to be an extremely delicate business. Cameras were for stark, formal family portraits surrounded by the most expensive objects in the house – a Chinese radio or a Swiss chocolate box sent by a relative in Bucharest fifteen years ago – and one must never, even at a wedding, smile. The idea of recording 'everyday reality' was regarded as ridiculous. It was especially comical that I should want to capture something so commonplace as the hand milking of a cow or the shearing of sheep, although important occasions

such as the killing of a pig were considered suitable. My
squeamishness during the latter ritual was a matter of great
hilarity – I would hide behind my camera lens pretending
that I wasn't really there as the throat was cut to great
cheers all around me.

My desire to photograph the filth and hardship of
peasant life often offended. It implied that I thought the
subject of my attentions particularly poor, which I found
increasingly frustrating since everyone moaned a great deal
about the harshness of their lives. But appearances were
important and no mother wanted it recorded on film that
she let her children run around in torn and grimy clothes,
just as no man wanted me to photograph the ribs sticking
from his underfed horse's side or the evidence that he could
not afford repairs to the collapsing roof of his home.

My possession of a camera, however, immediately gave
me VIP status at public events, and the lack of privacy
inherent in Romanian life meant that most major events
were public. An awful lot of people died in April and May,
apparently of natural causes, and it proved impossible to
pass through a village where a funeral was taking place
without joining in. I was immediately seated at the head
table alongside the priest, mayor and close family, fed
course after course of surprisingly good food (a pig was
often killed for the occasion) and asked endless questions
about myself. The deceased was rarely mentioned and my
enquiries were often answered in bemusement – since I
hadn't known him or her it was very strange of me to
show such concern.

The coffin would be positioned in the middle of all the
trestle tables where most of the village were eating. It was
still open, with the body dressed in his Sunday best, and
relatives were often sitting around it crying and wailing.
I was encouraged, even ordered, to take photographs
of their grief (it was taken for granted that I would
later send them the developed prints). After the meal

we would all be given special plaited round loaves, like going home presents, before forming a procession towards the graveyard. The now-covered coffin was usually carried in an ox-cart, with me positioned alongside to take all necessary photos until the poor chap was safely interred under several feet of soil.

The family would thank me profusely for coming and I never failed to feel honoured that I was allowed to share such private moments. But the instant privilege which was constantly bestowed upon me as a Westerner I found difficult to come to terms with: the racism and snobbery that I had been so appalled at during my first visit, I now realized I was inextricably caught up in and undoubtedly benefiting from. On the social scale, being British came somewhere very near the top; French or Italian may have been higher, but Britain's monarchy and the fact that it has not been successfully invaded since 1066 meant a great deal. What seemed to impress people most was Britain's amazing luck – in being an island, in having been industrialized for so long, and especially in its incredible good fortune in happening to have taken the winning side in both world wars.

I was constantly aware that my reception would have been entirely different had I been Black, Asian, Turkish, Hungarian, Russian, Gypsy, Jewish, Moslem . . . the list goes on. Of course the same is probably true of travelling anywhere, but I had never been made more aware of it. However, it didn't bother me as much as it had on my first visit because it was coming from people who had no reason to know better – their arguments were not meant to be in any way intellectually convincing and were clearly based on genuine fear. I was often asked if I had ever met someone from one of the above categories, and if I said yes there was always a fascinated enquiry as to what they were actually like. Were they really as awful as it was rumoured? It made it easy for me to do my bit for racial harmony as I said how my best friends were all from these groups and I painted a blissful picture of Britain as a haven for ethnic minorities. I apologize to all those who suffer for this not being true, but I was answering such comments as:

'Does Britain have black people?'

'Yes, quite a lot.'

'How *awful* for you!'

On the whole, politics meant little more than the price of the maize and flour they were unable to grow in the mountains. The revolution had brought a welcome end to taxation; in Communist times they had been forced to give a substantial proportion of what they produced to the state – meat, milk, wool, eggs. Now, in theory, they could sell their surplus on the open market. The trouble was that the nearest market was usually many miles away. For the time being most people seemed to be simply enjoying their new extras, knitting extra jumpers or splashing out on a feast of two pigs instead of one for a daughter's wedding. With the high inflation rate they understandably thought it stupid to convert a cow into cash; far better to keep it in preparation for the bad times that were bound to come, when it would be much more use than a new radio. There was a fatalistic acceptance that life would always be tough, and most didn't really seem to care about the revolution one way or the other. Rulers come, rulers go, and life goes on pretty much the same in the end. It would be great to have the possibilities of life in the West of course, and maybe it would happen one day if something marvellous happened like America taking over Russia, but a mere change of power within Romania itself wasn't going to make much difference.

Similarly, women appeared to accept their role in society with surprising calm and good humour. It was a feminist's nightmare, and the age at which girls married would have amounted to paedophilia in the West. In Maramuresh it was not uncommon for a girl to marry at fourteen, and I met women of my own age with anything up to six children already. They were the ones who asked me endless questions about my own life and my travels, as if feasting on it, and without exception younger women thought what I was doing was marvellous.

Their grandmothers found my not being married at the age of twenty-four infinitely more worrying. This could not possibly be a matter of choice and some of them set about the business of finding me a husband as a matter of urgency, telling me they knew of a suitable young man as if they were throwing me a life raft. If one of the latter had the misfortune of being present in the house he would be presented, squirming with embarrassment, for inspection.

'Do shut up, Granma,' he would protest. 'She's a Westerner, she wants someone rich and sophisticated.'

'Nonsense! There's nothing wrong with a good honest Romanian who works hard in the fields and believes in God – that's what counts, isn't it?' she would reply, turning to me for confirmation.

If I admitted that all five of the children in my family were still single, they would grow seriously worried and most concerned for my parents, so for an easier life my porkies began extending to this area too. I married off my elder sister and gave her a couple of children, to the great relief of the old women of Transylvania.

The way I wore jeans was something to be marvelled at by most of the women but was also a little shocking, so often I wore skirts so as not to offend anyone. Trousers coupled with my lack of a head scarf even managed to cause confusion as to my gender on one memorable occasion. An old lady asked me, most perplexed, whether I was a boy or a girl, and began feeling my breasts as if to make absolutely sure I was female.

Men were indulged and allowed to get away with

blue murder, mainly in the form of getting drunk. They often arrived home from work already well-intoxicated, expecting to be fed immediately before collapsing on to the bed by the fire. Some time later they would wake up and join in the general conversation, entirely remorseless and unapologetic. Saturday nights and Sundays were reserved especially for the process of inebriation and eventually I gave up trying to travel at the weekends, so full were the roads of drunken men stopping me for incomprehensible monologues. If I tried to move on they would grab me or the donkey, forcing me to listen while their friends roared with laughter a few yards away. At home their wives would quietly put up with them, putting them to bed when they finally staggered home, and keeping the children well out of the way.

During the many hours that I sat and talked with these women, I tried to bring up the subject of the orphanages. I found a great deal of genuine ignorance of their existence and they were usually horrified if I showed them the photographs in the magazine articles that I'd brought with me. With their network of extended families, they found it impossible to understand the reasons why a woman would give up her child into the care of anyone but a relative, and when I suggested that life in the cities was much harder for women trying to raise a family, I would be faced with that familiar look of disbelief. The cities were magical, luxurious places where hot water came on tap, where you could buy your children's clothes from a shop, without having to make them by hand. On the subject of handicapped children, I met the old Victorian attitude that they should not be allowed to survive after birth. Just as you would with an animal, if there was something wrong with it, it was not meant to be, so you should kill it. Furthermore, handicap was often a sign from God that the child was evil or that a spirit had laid a curse on it, or it might be a punishment for something the parents had done wrong. There was therefore nothing you could do to help such children and it was kinder to let them die.

Beliefs such as these, in God's magical powers and in a more basic form of sorcery abounded, although it was hard to catch anything but glimpses of it. Whenever I asked outright there would be an embarrassed silence followed by claims of 'Oh, no one believes in that nonsense any more'. Even so, nobody ever took a horse out without first attaching bright red tassels to its bridle. An old man explained to me that these ward off evil spirits and protect the horse from wolves and bears, although most people simply told me that to go out without them was unlucky.

A great deal of value was attached to my donkey's excreta. We were calmly plodding along the outskirts of a village one day, when a woman of about forty rushed up to me with a bag, asking me if she could have some of Hannibal's '*caca*' since her daughter was very ill. My look of bewilderment produced the explanation that she intended to make tea with it and feed it to her daughter so as to make the fever go down, and she appeared amazed that I did not know about this simple remedy. When I suggested that it might be easier for her to collect droppings from the many horses in the village rather than walk with me until Hannibal decided to make a bowel movement, she informed me that donkey droppings are much, much more effective than horse droppings. Donkeys, you see, are holy animals who once carried Christ to the Cross; they therefore have special healing powers, hence the reason why donkeys so rarely fall ill themselves.

She accompanied us for twenty minutes until Hannibal obliged with some perfectly formed specimens. Similar requests were made so often over the following weeks that I began keeping samples ready prepared in the cart so as to save my clientele the trouble of having to wait.

A custom I found everywhere, even in the towns, was that of swaddling babies so that their legs are held straight together and their arms tightly bound next to their bodies. They were unable to move at all, apart from the brief moments of freedom at nappy changing time when their limbs would burst into frantic movement as if making up for lost time. They are kept like this for their first year, the idea being to prevent their growing up physically deformed. If their legs were allowed to grow in the splayed outward direction in which they appear at birth, the child would not be able to walk in later life. In remoter parts, babies' faces are also bound for the first six weeks of life, to be seen only at feeding time. This so to say prevents them from being ugly and from their heads growing in a strange shape.

The consequence of this was that babies and toddlers are remarkably fat and wobbly. They had practically no muscle tone, and because they were kept inside all day they looked pale and horribly unhealthy, considering all the trouble their parents were taking to prevent their physical deformity. Whenever I commented that these practices were long ago given up in the West – my mother hadn't bound me up, and I hadn't turned out too much of a monster, had I? – I met with nothing but embarrassed excuses that they were merely doing what had been common sense for generations, and anyway, we had medicines in the West to stop deformities whereas they had to rely on more traditional methods.

This presumption that Western medicines could cure anything and everything was widespread, and there was general shock that anyone in the West ever became ill at all. I added considerably to this belief by my wearing of contact lenses. They were the object of endless fascination; older people were often frightened of them and asked me to take them out whilst we were talking, while others with bad eyesight insisted I let them try them on, not understanding that there could be different kinds of lenses for different eye defects.

In the mountains making up the border between

Maramuresh and the Transylvanian region of Bistritsa, I met an extremely attractive and modern lady doctor who was battling against beliefs such as these in her role as a GP. She covered an enormous area of isolated farms and settlements. I met her on a small track one afternoon as she squeezed past us in a very old and battered van which had '*salvatsul*' – ambulance – written on the side. She was blonde, wore make-up and jeans, and for a moment I thought I was dreaming – I hadn't seen a woman look like that for months. She explained that she was the doctor in the village of Tirlishua down in one of the valleys and she invited me to stay the night, hurriedly scribbling directions on to a piece of paper before crunching the van into gear and driving on.

I arrived four hours later in a somewhat bedraggled state, owing to William, my Dobermann, having chased a cat into the small river on the outskirts of the village and my having dived in after them. This turned out to be a blessing in disguise, for I was given a bath – my first since setting off from England. A wood-fired boiler was stoked up and an hour later I soaked in an old enamel tub, feeling almost drunk from the sensation of piping hot water and creamy soap (mine) on skin.

The doctor was called Edit and she came from Baia Mare, a large city in the north-western corner of the country. She had been assigned to this district, in the way that all doctors were assigned to their posts before the revolution unless they had the connections to ensure their own personal choice. There had once been four doctors working from the Tirlishua clinic but since the revolution the others had all emigrated, two to Germany and one to Israel. Now that doctors had the freedom to apply for whatever jobs they wanted, no one had come to fill their places and as Edit showed me around the clinic, I understood why. I was appalled that any doctor should be expected to work in such conditions – the place was literally falling to pieces. The tools of her trade were an archaic collection that in Britain would belong in a museum. She had just two needles that she sterilized in a pot in her own kitchen, a collection of bandages worn wafer thin from repeated boiling, and she showed me the pathetic array of medicines that she was allocated each month by central Government.

On top of this, Edit claimed that her greatest problems were witchcraft and priests. Most of the people in her five hundred square kilometre area came to her only as a last resort, when their strange potions and their pleas for God's intervention had failed, by which time there was often very little she could do. She would sometimes have to force her way into a house where she knew someone was very ill; and she rarely had enough confidence in her patients taking their pills voluntarily to be able to leave medicines with them, resulting in her having to make sometimes thrice-daily visits to isolated houses so that she could actually witness the drugs being swallowed. She said she often felt more like a vet than a doctor as she trudged for hours up mud tracks impenetrable to cars. Once, she told me, she had to deliver a breech birth in a house without water or electricity, where the animals were kept indoors at night and she'd had to resort to washing her hands in their drinking trough.

Edit was paid 4,500 *lei* a month – about 11 pounds. With this she had to pay for any repairs to the clinic and for the diesel she needed beyond the tiny allowance she received from the state to drive around the area. She talked to me about the nightmare of having to play God: her supplies of medicines were so limited that she had to choose between equally needy patients, forced to give priority to the young over the old, unable to 'waste' medicine on relieving the pain of those who were dying if it could save the lives of others.

Edit and her husband Gheorge, a Transylvanian of

Hungarian descent, had applied to emigrate to Hungary; she was concerned that this would leave Tirlishua and its surroundings without a doctor at all but I hoped for her sake that they made it. In the Ceauşescu years Hungarians had been treated very badly and it was not politically correct for a Romanian to marry one of them. After university Edit and Gheorge, an engineer, had been assigned to opposite ends of the country, 1,000 kilometres apart, even though they already had a baby daughter and had been married for three years. They spent all their money on train fares and for four years their marriage survived on monthly visits; for them the revolution had been a true saviour, enabling Gheorge to apply for a job in Bistritsa where he now worked.

A few days later I passed through the pretty Saxon town of Bistritsa, stopping to gorge myself on real Dutch-made Mars Bars that I found at a kiosk. There were also Western cigarettes, which were so mild I couldn't taste them after the three pence a packet Romanian-made 'Carpats' brand that I'd been smoking for the past month. Otherwise Bistritsa held few delights. Both Hannibal and I were terrified of the sudden heavy traffic; people stared without smiling or introducing themselves, and the reality of life in towns came back to me.

We escaped towards the Birgau Valley and, with my nose buried in a novel, I grew increasingly excited about what lay ahead. The book was *Dracula* and we were approaching the mountain range where Bram Stoker based the count's exploits; indeed, I was walking along the very road where Jonathan Harper first sensed his impending doom as passers-by crossed themselves upon hearing of his intended destination. As a joke I had purchased a string of garlic bulbs in Bistritsa and hung them on the entrance of my cart, but I was somewhat alarmed when more than one person I met told me it was a very sensible move if I planned to travel alone up to the top of the valley. My sense of apprehension was further increased by an horrendous attack of food poisoning after I'd eaten a meal at an isolated house up a steep track on the northern valley slopes. As I retched continually throughout the night I grew convinced that I had been poisoned.

Bram Stoker had chosen his location well; as we climbed higher we became surrounded by dense, dark forests of pine, rising into steep peaks on both sides. The road twisted endlessly upwards; Hannibal was wonderful, pulling the cart up over 2,000 feet in a day, strangely not wanting to stop for the frequent rests that he usually demanded in such conditions. I'd been warned on no account to stop and camp in the forests, since my donkey would certainly be eaten by either bears or wolves. I'd seen enough of the results of bear and wolf attacks to know that such warnings were not made in jest – horses with great chunks missing from their legs (horses were such a valuable commodity that, if they survived the attack, once the wounds had healed they had to keep working, often hobbling along at a painfully slow pace), and a sheep dog who had lost an eye fighting off a wolf that was decimating his flock. Men would sometimes proudly show me their scars or boast of when they had killed a bear, a greatly feared animal. Officially bear hunting was illegal but I saw many of the huge furry skins hung up on living-room walls or in more practical use as bed covers. I alternated between my longing to see one of these majestic creatures for real and my dread of being killed. I only ever heard a wolf once, in Maramuresh as I camped wild in a wooded valley; its howl was unmistakable, almost corny, just like something from a Wild West film. It woke me up at two o'clock in the morning and I was absolutely terrified, even though it must have been miles away. I stoked up the fire and kept it blazing till dawn, unable to sleep.

Back in Dracula's Birgau pass, we managed to reach the hotel near the top before nightfall. The hotel was built as a tourist attraction at the height of the Communist madness; it is meant to be a replica of Dracula's castle, but somehow they managed to build a modern-looking concrete nightmare that looks more like a prison than a castle. A ski lift stands next to it, rising to the high southern slopes that were still covered with snow in May, but no cable was ever put in it so it has never actually been used in the five years since the tourist complex was created.

Nevertheless, the hotel staff proved to be the friendliest and most helpful of any that I found in Romania – I was even charged simple Romanian prices without having to fight about it. Food and accommodation was provided for all of us, the animals in the garages and me in a fine twin bedroom with blood-red walls and a nest of crows outside the tiny window, who kept beating against the glass all night and frightening the hell out of me.

I had heard that somewhere nearby were the ruins of a real castle, so the next day I gave Hannibal a rest and set out with the dogs to find it. I found unbelievably isolated houses, their occupiers out on the Alpine slopes cutting hay, but none of them had a clue about a castle and had certainly never heard of Dracula. I contented myself with climbing up above the snow line and building an ice statue of what turned into an extremely well-endowed Queen Victoria.

Beyond the hotel lay the border between Transylvania and Moldavia, and as I stood at the top of the pass I could see nothing but pine-covered mountains with snow-capped peaks in all directions. Over the next few weeks, as I made my way eastwards, I saw the prettiest, fairy-tale villages. These were noticeably wealthier – with strong timber houses covered in ornately carved wooden tiles – than those in the bare hills the other side of Bistritsa. I noticed a change in the people, too. Greater prosperity meant more televisions and modern dress, with an increased awareness of the outside world. I'm still not sure whether it was a regional difference or merely because of the sudden arrival of spring, but my diet improved drastically. Suddenly there were spring onions and radishes on the table; with the new-born calves came a glut of frantic cheesemaking, and sour cream was added to all the soups and stews. By the end of May *slanina* appeared only in my nightmares and I could enjoy mealtimes in sobriety.

I zigzagged through the mountains, but every few days I was forced to follow a section of the busy highway running along the main valley floor. The traffic was predominantly from the Soviet Union – East Moldavians taking advantage of the newly relaxed border controls to visit relatives and to sell heavily subsidized goods from their own state-owned shops in the markets. Time and time again I was presumed to be Russian and was asked what I had for sale; at times it drove me bananas as people grabbed my clothes and my pots from the cart, yelling '*Cit costa? Cit costa?*'

Much of the other traffic consisted of aid trucks, great thundering freighters from Germany, France, Scandinavia . . . The British ones I tried to flag down to beg for goodies such as instant coffee or tea bags, but often the drivers merely waved back and got out their cameras, presuming me to be just another revolting peasant. Their presence was not lost on the villagers, whose resentment of their passing on through without giving them any aid was enormous. Over and over again I was told of the injustice of the orphans getting everything when the ordinary people had nothing; as they saw it, their own children were in rags while little gypsy bastards were dressed in the donations from the best fashion houses of Europe. They'd recently been told on the radio that over a hundred million dollars' worth of that magical stuff known as '*ajutoare*' – humanitarian aid – had come into the country since the revolution.

'And what have we seen of it? Absolutely nothing, that's what, and it isn't bloody fair.'

It was so unfair that I heard swear words being used for

the first time outside of extreme drunkenness. I was in a rather difficult position since I seemed to stand accused along with all other Westerners. My attempts to justify the concentration of efforts on the orphanages never did any good, so usually I sympathized and said I would see what I could do to influence the aid organizations when I returned home, which went down very well.

Thus I tried to stay away from the villages on the valley floor, and after the constant dialogue and lack of privacy of the past weeks I enjoyed the solitude of the hills, lighting great fires to see off the bears and wolves. Unfortunately, and perhaps predictably, the only attack I suffered was of a human kind. In a way I am loath to include it, since every country has its madmen and the incident was a one-off, entirely different from the treatment I received from everyone else on my travels. But the aftermath showed that it shocked other people just as much, perhaps more than it did me, and the kindness I received afterwards touched me deeply.

Whenever I camped wild I met 'chobani', shepherds who roam the hills for weeks at a time with their flocks of sheep and goats and their huge dogs, the latter trained not for herding but for seeing off predators. Often they had donkeys with them to carry the provisions, tiny animals half Hannibal's size who would 'eeyore' in delight upon seeing him as if greeting a long-lost relation. The shepherds had always been friendly and gentlemanly, stopping to share my camp-fires and treating me almost as one of their own kind, then pouring me a glass of their *tsuica* as they commented that I must own a big herd at home to warrant a donkey of such size. As I prepared for bed they would take their leave and wish me luck, calling their dogs and continuing on their way to wherever it was they planned to spend the night.

On this particular evening my camp was in an idyllic spot, by the side of a stream at the edge of the tree line.

I'd left a village about two miles below me down a small track, and the next day I planned to cross an uninhabited mountain area. I had just prepared my supper and was about to eat when a tall young man with blond hair and a moustache came down the hill along the track. Spotting my camp he walked over – there was nothing unusual in this and I hailed a greeting. He told me he was a shepherd and came from the other side of the mountains. I said that I was heading that way and asked him about the area.

Even when he began persistently questioning me about my marital state, I wasn't unduly worried – again, it was nothing out of the ordinary. Gradually it became apparent that he was putting himself forward as a candidate, and twenty minutes after meeting me he proposed marriage. He had a flock of sheep, I had a donkey – we were made for each other, and since we both had blue eyes and fair hair, apparently we would make beautiful babies.

I confess to having laughed, which didn't go down well. He would not take no for an answer and it dawned on me that he might actually be serious. I grew worried and set about trying to get rid of him. I managed it after twenty minutes, but not without him calling me a bitch and a tease and a stuck-up foreigner who didn't think he was good enough. When he finally left along the track to the village I heaved a sigh of relief and re-heated my supper.

Half an hour later it was dark and I went to bed. The sky had promised rain so I had put up my tent – the cart was too small to keep me, my belongings and the dogs dry at the same time, unless I spent all night crouched into a small ball. As usual after a long day's walk, I fell asleep immediately and I had no idea what the time was when I woke up suddenly. Something heavy had fallen on the tent, and my immediate fear was of an avalanche. I listened and heard nothing; no rumbling or snapping of twigs. Then it happened again – wham, a heavy stone landed against the side of the tent, hitting Georgie on the side. She yelped furiously. The stones kept coming at regular intervals. One sharp rock ripped through the fly sheet, just missing my head, and I grew terrified. Who the hell was out there? What did they want?

I tried to send the dogs out to see the intruders off, but even William refused to go. They just sat looking as confused and frightened as I was.

Eventually I had to get out myself when one of the missiles pulled out the front guy rope and the tent nearly collapsed. I grabbed William by the collar and forced him to come out with me. A stone hit my shin and I screamed, trying desperately to think of what to do. Trying to turn my fear into something more positive and keeping a tight hold on William's collar, I began shouting in the direction I thought the missiles were coming from. My Romanian had never been so fluent as I yelled out into the darkness.

'What do you want? If you want something from me, come and talk to me,' (anything to stop these stones coming at me), 'but I warn you, I have a dog who'll kill you if you lay a finger on me.'

My fierce Dobermann, however, was trying desperately to get away from me as more and more stones hit us. Georgie had long since disappeared, and an unwanted quiver had entered my voice as I continued shouting. It was impossible to know where the stones were coming from – somewhere in the trees above me, but more precisely I couldn't tell. I ordered whoever it was to leave immediately or I would set my dog on him. I shone my torch around and began marching up and down the foot of the trees, blasting out my orders, but when a large stone hit my shoulder I couldn't help yelling out in pain. I felt desperate.

As I shone the torch behind a tree I saw a pair of eyes. A man was cowering underneath the branches, his arm shielding his face, and suddenly I thought I'd made a mistake – this was some innocent passer-by who had been terrified by my threats and thought I was going to kill him. I stood back and gestured to him to come out – and it was then that I screamed. He came rushing towards me, and in his hand was a sharp rock, held high as though he were about to bring it crashing down on my head. As I turned and ran I was vaguely aware of William bolting ahead of me into the darkness.

It was the shepherd whom I'd been speaking to just before, and his eyes were crazy. I panicked – I was convinced that he wanted to kill me. It was like one of those nightmares where you're running to get away from someone but your feet refuse to move. He was between me and the track so I had to go the other way, into the stream, where my espadrilles came off in the water. I just couldn't run fast enough. I screamed and screamed, praying that someone would hear me as I floundered from rock to rock. Suddenly he was in front of me: he must have overtaken me and was waiting for me to effectively stumble into his arms. I dropped the torch and turned, heading up for the tracks. I'd hardly gone ten yards when I felt a hand on my shoulder and then suddenly I was on the ground, him on top of me, his arm in the air with the same rock in his hand, about to come crashing down on my skull.

It's true – your whole life does flash before you. Or rather you become extremely philosophical about the prospect of imminent death. I was vaguely aware of this being a bloody awful, stupid way to go, stuck in the middle of Romania being clobbered by a mad shepherd. I thought of my parents and apologized for putting them through such needless pain – I should have been a barrister after all. If I was going to die young I wanted it to be heroic, so that my folks could be proud, not like this. And where the hell was my dog? I was travelling with a huge Dobermann for Christ's sake – a great deal of use he'd turned out to be in my hour of need.

His left hand was round my neck and his right hand with

the rock in it was coming down. I shut my eyes. Suddenly his mouth was on mine, his tongue was in my mouth, and relief flooded through me. Thank God, thank God, I repeated over and over in my head – he just wants to rape me, he doesn't want to kill me after all. As an alternative it was truly wonderful: I'd let him do anything to me as long as he didn't kill me. My body went limp and I just lay there as he undid his belt, feeling strangely detached, my mind working overtime concentrating on crazy details such as the fact that because I wasn't struggling I'd never be able to prove in court that I had been raped. I'd never realized before quite how stupid this condition is – when you think you're going to be killed you don't do anything to provoke it. He still had the rock in his hand and I knew that if I struggled he was more than likely to use it. I kept praying that he wasn't going to kill me afterwards, that he would let me be once he'd finished, and I certainly wasn't going to do anything to provoke him to further violence.

Then, in an instant, we were rolling over – someone else seemed to have joined in. I hit my head against something hard and as I was thrown out of my detachment I felt hopelessly confused. I could feel claws digging into me. William! I suddenly clicked that it was a dog – *my* dog – and he had hold of the man's elbow in his jaws. At last I realized that it was safe to struggle and I pulled myself free, scrambling to my feet and racing up towards the track.

I have never run as fast or been less aware of self-inflicted pain. I didn't dare stop to look back in case he was right behind me. The dogs both joined me after about five minutes and together we fled towards the village. It seemed to take forever. I kept thinking that at any moment I'd feel his hand on my shoulder again. At the first house we came to I ran up to the entrance and began beating against the door. After what felt like an eternity it was opened by an old couple in their night clothes and it was then, with safety staring at me in the face, that I crumpled. Suddenly I began sobbing. I couldn't even stand up and I sank down to the ground, hugging on to my knees, unable to say a single word.

The old people took a shoulder each and pulled me inside, sitting me down on a chair by the fire, asking me what had happened, telling me they'd seen me pass through the village earlier in the afternoon. I felt their eyes wander over my body and suddenly I noticed my filthy, torn pyjamas, my bare feet raw and bleeding. I was shaking uncontrollably and it was another few minutes before I could make myself understood.

It wasn't until the old man mentioned it that I realized I'd left all my valuables – my passport, camera, money supply – in the tent. I couldn't actually give a damn about them, I was feeling so lucky to be alive, but Jacob and Agappia insisted that they be fetched. I explained the whereabouts of my camp and Jacob rode up there with his son, Marin, who by now had come downstairs with his wife to see what all the commotion was about. They armed themselves with stakes and looked ready for battle. When they returned half an hour later they almost seemed disappointed that it had all been quiet – Hannibal had even been asleep, they said. Luckily my stuff was untouched. They had brought back my money belt and camera with them, saying they'd seen nothing at all, and as they began questioning me in greater detail, I began to wonder whether I'd dreamt the whole thing. Agappia kept saying that she didn't believe it, no one round here would behave like that – and it was true, now that I was back in the safety of a normal Romanian home, the whole story seemed extremely unlikely.

The next morning, however, when I went back up the valley with Marin to fetch Hannibal and the rest of my belongings, it all came back to me with horrible clarity as I saw all the stones around the tent and found my torch in the stream. When we returned to the village I discovered that Jacob hadn't doubted my word, for he was waiting for us in the house with the local policeman. Part of me wanted to run away – this was making it more real, and I didn't want it to be, I just wanted to forget, to pretend it hadn't happened.

Jacob had told most of the story already, and I only had to add a few details. The policeman kept apologizing to me, saying how ashamed he was that this had happened, promising that they would find the culprit and punish him. Jacob had said nothing to me but it seemed that he had a pretty good idea of who the blond shepherd was, and the policeman said he'd be in touch soon when they'd caught him.

Thus I ended up staying with Jacob and Agappia for over a week. Each morning I tried to leave, saying that they'd never find him and I couldn't stay with them forever, but Agappia would insist that I had to wait another day and deep down I was grateful. My confidence had been shattered and the prospect of setting out on my own was terrifying. To stay at home with Agappia, letting her teach me how to make cheese and spin wool, copying the patterns of my jumpers that she liked on to paper so that she could knit them, was the best therapy in the world. They even let my dogs come inside, which was something unheard of in most Romanian households.

On the morning of the fourth day, Victor, the policeman, arrived saying that I must come to the local dairy at once to identify my attacker. The suspect had apparently arrived with a milk delivery at dawn and was now being held by the depot manager.

During the twenty minute journey Victor explained to me my options if the man turned out to be the right one. We could prosecute formally through the courts, but this could take months and I would have to remain in the area throughout. Victor suspected rightly that I was not keen to do this, but there was an alternative, he said. We could get a written confession from him and impose a fine, in the form of a contract between him and myself, enforceable by law. I said yes. I wanted him behind bars but I knew I had next to no evidence and a court case would probably achieve nothing. A foreigner being involved in a case of attempted rape would undoubtedly involve the press, ruining my future travels and making me notorious for something that I just wanted to forget. And I'd heard enough about Romanian prisons to know that he would not come out of one a more stable person than when he went in – it would probably be just the thing he needed to turn him into a successful rapist and murderer.

So I said yes to the fine option and as we walked into the dairy, a large building at the side of the main road, the policeman sensed my fear and took my arm. He had been a perfect gentleman throughout and had never once suggested that I should not have been camping in the mountains on my own. In fact no one had even hinted that I had been to blame in any way, and I was constantly impressed by that: instead it was apparently a matter of national pride that a foreigner should be able to travel safely in Romania and everyone in the village seemed almost personally affronted when they heard what had happened.

This reaction was acted out inside the dairy building. I was introduced to the manager and sat down at the desk in his office as the suspect was brought in. As I recognized him I burst into tears and began shaking uncontrollably again. I nodded affirmation when the policeman asked me, somewhat unnecessarily, if this was indeed the man who had attacked me, and then I watched as Victor set on him in very genuine rage, sending him flying around the room as he called him every filthy name I'd ever heard of.

My own feelings consisted of little more than desperately wanting to get out of the room. I recognized his smell more than anything and it brought it all back. As Victor made him grovel on his knees before me, apologizing, I couldn't even bring myself to look at him. I wanted Victor to beat him to a pulp but I didn't want to see it. I was vaguely aware of him signing a piece of paper admitting his guilt and promising to pay a fine of 10,000 *lei* by the following Friday, and then he left.

On the way back to Jacob and Agappia's we stopped off at the local mayor's office, so that Victor could inform him of the latest developments and because the mayor apparently wanted to apologize to me in person for what had happened whilst I was staying in his district. The two men plied me with *tsuica* and even brought out a bar of chocolate, a luxury I hadn't seen for months. The sell-by date on the back of the packet said 1989, but it tasted pretty good. I ended up spending the afternoon playing backgammon with them. Villagers kept coming in – they had all heard who I was and what had happened – and wishing me well, saying how shocked and sorry they were.

'And it was one of us, not even a gypsy! The shame of it!'

The shepherd didn't turn up with his fine on the Friday and the police discovered that he hadn't been seen by his employer (it had not been true about him owning his own flock) since his interrogation at the dairy. He had fled, which didn't increase my confidence about setting out on my travels once more and convinced me that I'd made the wrong choice about not prosecuting him formally – if I heard that he'd attacked someone else I'd never forgive myself. But there was little I could do about it now and I had to leave it in the hands of the police. I instructed Victor to give the money to Jacob and Agappia if ever they found him and managed to extract the fine, and on the Sunday I set off, feeling terrified but knowing I couldn't stay in the safety of Jacob and Agappia's lovely home forever.

I welcomed the busy main road and I never again spent a night alone in the cart or my tent, thanking God for the endless offers of a bed for the night. In the stretches between villages I saw my attacker behind every rock, hiding in every tree, and I began taking rides in horse carts, hitching Hannibal on behind, so that I wasn't alone. The lack of privacy that had annoyed me before was suddenly a wonderful thing. Sharing a bed was the best way to get a good night's sleep, and I joined in everyday village life again with renewed vigour.

Throughout my travels I found myself inundated with gifts: pieces of elaborately embroidered cloth, chunks of *slanina* to keep me going on my journey, even hand-knitted jumpers. I became frightened of admiring anything for fear of it being immediately wrapped up and presented to me; like the food I was given, it was considered insulting to refuse, implying that I didn't like it. And my thanks were usually considered over the top; if they could make or obtain more of the same, they thought it perfectly reasonable for me to ask if I could have it. Though such an attitude provided me with a wonderful collection of genuine hand-made Romanian goods, it made life rather difficult regarding my own possessions.

I had brought with me a collection of soaps and shampoos which I knew were luxuries to give as presents to those who offered me hospitality. I usually gave them as soon as I'd arrived, and on departure I would leave a few dollar bills wrapped up in a thank-you note. However, on numerous occasions my hosts would ask me if they could have a shirt or a jersey that they had spotted in my bag and which they particularly liked; sometimes I discovered that an item of clothing had simply disappeared, taken by the same people who had just shown me the utmost kindness and generosity. It proved extremely difficult saying 'no' and asking for them back; they would offer to give back the soap or shampoo, saying how they liked my shirt so much more and, after all, I could always get another one

– they knew that, because I came from the West and you can buy anything in the West. I couldn't believe how guilty I was made to feel for wanting to keep hold of my own extremely limited wardrobe. I eventually discovered a way round it – everything I owned became a present from a loved one. Presents are sacred and not to be given away, and in that case of course they understood.

In the hills of Bukovina I came across a group of people whose friendliness surpassed all that I'd encountered before. In the small town at the bottom of the valley I'd been told that up in the hills were three settlements of 'foreigners', but few knew more than that; some said they were Czechs, some thought they were Poles, all confirmed that they had a 'strange' religion. I was fascinated and I went up there to see what I might find.

I'm still not sure why I liked them so much. Almost everyone I'd met so far had been incredibly friendly but the Bukovina Poles seemed quite simply overjoyed to see me, thrilled that I should be visiting them – and not because I was a foreigner and something new, but rather because I was one of them, that is *not* a Romanian. They used 'us and them' terminology when speaking of the Romanians and I was clearly in the 'us' category.

They lived in three small, very isolated villages. Although their ancestors had left Poland nearly 200 years ago, they had vigorously kept hold of their language and their religion. Most knew Romanian but at home they spoke Polish. Apparently it was a very antiquated form; the year before a group of the younger people had made a trip to relatives in Poland and they had found it very hard to make themselves understood.

They were Catholics and this more than anything else separated them from mainstream Romanian life. Since Christmas I had tried to keep away from priests, although their centrality to village life often brought me into contact with them and if a priest invited me to stay at his house all other offers usually quietly vanished. But here, amongst these stranded Polish settlers, I saw a faith that was a positive driving force quite unlike anything I'd experienced before. I even found myself enjoying a bout of quite uncharacteristic religious fervour as I attended mass with them. The churches and the priests' houses were run-down and dilapidated, and I loved them for it. They were at one with their communities and I saw a spiritual beauty that had been lacking elsewhere in the villages where the church was the one building displaying wealth and luxury.

The Catholic priests of these Polish villages were amongst the most remarkable men I have ever met. One of the three had spent many years in political prisons; they were all highly educated men and all were vehement in their attacks on past and present Romanian leaders, in a way that was more informative than any books and articles I had read. I stayed with two of them and on both occasions we stayed up talking late into the night. What was so impressive was the way they complained most strongly not about ill treatment of Catholics under Communism (although life had by no means been easy for them), but about how the Uniate Church had been completely annihilated. The Catholics had always had Rome to fight for them, they said, just as Protestants had powerful German backing, but the Uniate Church had had no one.

The Uniate Church was created during the Hungarian occupation of Transylvania in an attempt to undermine the religious independence of the Romanians. It was a strange compromise between Orthodoxy and Catholicism, whereby they stuck to the main tenet of Orthodoxy that holds there is no division between God, the Son and the Holy Ghost, but they recognized the Pope as their spiritual leader and God's chosen prophet. At the time of the Second World War there were reckoned to be three million Uniate Church members in Romania. The Communists banned the faith outright, their churches were handed over to mainstream Orthodox priests, and Uniates were imprisoned unless they renounced their faith. Catholic and Protestant priests were permitted to practise as long as they said nothing negative about the Government; their congregations were usually denied promotions and privileges in their normal lives but were permitted to go to church as often as they liked, whereas the Uniates were arrested even for clandestine prayer at home. Since the revolution they'd been trying to get their churches back, but Orthodox priests were of course unwilling to hand them over. These Catholic priests I met in Moldavia were trying to persuade their own leadership in Rome to fight on the Uniate Church's behalf, and I was impressed. If this was how the Catholic Church had behaved in Poland during the Communist years, no wonder the Poles were finding the transition to democracy easier than the Romanians.

In fact, one of the priests was sure that the religious Orthodoxy of Romania and Bulgaria was the reason why they were so far behind the other countries of Eastern Europe in embracing democracy and reform. Ironically, though, he took his argument back to the Reformation – Russia and her Orthodox neighbours took no part in the liberating process that spread through Catholic Europe in the 16th century, with its consequential questioning of the social and political order. Romanians, he said, are not used to making up their own minds about anything; he likened them to small children whose cruel, strict father has just died, leaving them penniless. They have just been told that the world is now their oyster, but even the best of them have no experience of anything but following orders and trying to keep out of trouble.

A few days after this I spent a night amongst another ethnic minority that similarly treated me as one of their own – the gypsies. I had seen far fewer gypsies on my travels than I had expected, and I had been warned about their evil ways so often by people that I was inevitably influenced and felt frightened if I met them in large numbers – for they were indeed very different. So far I had come across them only in the grim outskirts of towns, living in the worst housing, and I was inundated with pleas for charity – for clothes or food, and usually money. But this time I met some real travelling gypsies. They were camped by the side of a track, in two shabby wagons, and they invited me to join them. I had a long walk ahead of me to the next village and I was loath to camp alone, so I accepted the invitation and parked Hannibal alongside their three horses. There were seven adults and umpteen children; the women and girls were dressed in wonderful, brightly coloured skirts, their hair was long and plaited, and they wore great gold loops in their ears. I watched them, fascinated, but it was the men who did most of the talking as we sat around their fire eating a potato stew. They were heading for Yash, the capital of Moldavia. No, they said, they didn't have a home, although they had settled relatives whom they stayed with from time to time. They made a living by selling what they could at market – cloth that they bought cheaply from 'contacts' and wooden goods such as spoons, clothes' hangers and rolling pins that the women carved by hand. Occasionally, they made forays into Hungary or the Soviet Union to purchase goods that were scarce within Romania, but this wasn't so profitable now that the border restrictions had lessened – everyone else was doing it. Before the revolution they had had an easier time than most Romanians in being able to travel abroad – 'They didn't want us anyway, they were quite happy to let us go'.

I was almost disappointed, as slowly the fearful mystery surrounding them was broken down. They were Orthodox Christians; most gypsies are nowadays, they said, and very few believe in the old pagan gods. They do have a chief though – they described him as being like a king – who lives in Transylvania and is their spiritual leader. They spoke of the 'special power' of gypsies, but as I asked them about it in greater detail it became clear that this was a device for scaring Romanians more than anything else. Yes, they said, there are some gypsies who have the power to see the future and to lay curses on people, who know many magic remedies and treatments. None of them claimed to have these powers, although they laughed and said that if they were abused by a Romanian they would always shout a curse back at them, just for effect. They had few illusions about the way they were seen by mainstream society: 'They think we are animals; they would kill us all if they could.' As regards the accusations of stealing and murder that I had heard so often, they were astonishingly honest. While saying they would never kill – they were Christians, it was wrong – they admitted to petty theft; since they weren't treated as human beings, they didn't see why they had to act honestly towards a society from which they felt totally alienated. They were adamant that they would never steal from a fellow gypsy, however – this could bring a curse on you or your family and, besides, gypsies had to stick together. This was their greatest criticism of the virtual extinction of travelling as the gypsy mode of life – as gypsies settled into fixed abodes, they were beginning to treat each other as only Romanians should be treated.

They knew I wasn't a real gypsy – I simply didn't look like one – but my method of travelling meant that they treated me in a way that I never experienced when I later met other gypsies as a normal Westerner. They did not ask for anything from me and I felt totally safe; whilst I was with them I was clearly regarded as one of them, by both them and the Romanians I met the next day. Word had got about that I had been camping with gypsies and as I passed through the next village I experienced hostility and unfriendliness for the first time.

'Are you what gypsies look like in England?'

'Yes,' I replied, since it was true – British gypsies do not look Indian as Romanian ones do.

'Well you're not welcome – we've got enough here already, we don't need more of your kind.'

It was by now almost June and I was slowly approaching Yonashen, the orphanage on the far side of the River Suchava. I was looking forward to getting there, but couldn't imagine what it would be like. The way of life that I had so far experienced in Romania was so completely family orientated that the idea of an institution was entirely alien. My conceptions of how Yonashen would be were drawn almost exclusively from what I had seen and read in the British press – those horrific pictures of row upon row of children in bare cots, covered in flies, banging their heads against the wall . . . But it didn't seem at all real, and I couldn't fit the various pictures together into a coherent idea of what daily life in an orphanage would be like. The British aid workers I imagined to be a rather serious bunch, and I feared that they'd disapprove of me and the way I'd been lazily gadding about the mountains with my donkey and cart whilst they were hard at work.

My arrival at Yonashen was delayed somewhat by the relentless rain that hit Moldavia at the end of May, holing me up at Gura Humorlui for a week and resulting in the collapse of the bridge I was planning to cross over the River Suchava. I was forced to travel many kilometres south into the city of Suchava – it was a nightmare of a day, as I tried to make my way through the industrial area towards the bridge. Rain poured down and Hannibal as usual refused to walk through any puddles, while hordes of people gathered round us asking what I had for sale, grabbing what they could from my cart. I ended up covering all my possessions with a blanket and sitting the dogs on top of it, and Hannibal and I plodded our way through the downpour.

I had about 30 kilometres left to go so I tried to keep Hannibal plodding for as long as I could that day in order to reach the orphanage by the end of the next. Consequently I refused all offers of a bed for the night until dusk fell, when all the offers dried up and I was faced with the unusual prospect of actually having to ask. We had just reached a village on the main north road and I was directed to the house of the priest.

'He'll give you a bed for the night,' I was told, and when I arrived I found a jolly old man with a white beard who said of course I could stay. There had been a wedding and the small house was full of people; I joined in and it was not until after ten o'clock that I was told where I would be staying. I was surprised to discover that, along with three other girls of about my own age, I would be sleeping on the floor of the priest's own room, around his large wooden bed. As we gathered at the table in the room to drink coffee and eat cakes, I noticed that the other girls all seemed a little odd – they kept talking about their 'demons' and would come out with occasional shrieks. One of them was a nun; she was quieter than the others and grew increasingly nervous as the meal progressed. The priest then explained to me that all the girls 'had the devil inside them' and they were staying with him for 'treatment'. He was renowned for his success at removing demons from people's heads, he said – he had even treated the daughter of a Minister some years ago for which he claimed Presidential recognition. His patients were sent from not only all over Romania, he said, but from Russia too.

When we had finished eating, the priest asked me if I'd like to stay and watch the 'treatment' taking place. I nodded and stayed glued to my seat as one of the girls, Maria, lay down on the floor. The priest took off his shoes and began walking over her body; Maria shrieked and the priest began yelling at her as he stomped over her breasts, her ribs, her stomach, her pubic bone.

'Out, devil, out! Where is the devil inside you? I challenge him to come forth from your body – let him fight me who has the strength to see him off!'

'No, no!' the girl screamed back as the priest shook her head up and down with his foot. 'My devil likes it here – he's in my head and in my heart and he won't leave me!'

'Tell me how he manifests himself!'

'He speaks to me, he encourages me to think wicked, sinful things. But he's my friend, I don't want him to leave!'

'You do! You do!' cried the priest as he jumped up and down.

I still only have to think about all this and I'm rendered as speechless as I was at the time. I was frightened as well – I wanted to take him off her, to stop him doing it, before running and getting the hell out of the place. But it was approaching midnight by now and I had nowhere to go. I sat there and tried to think what I could do to stop it, making feeble protestations such as 'But you're hurting her!' that were simply ignored as both priest's and girl's passions became increasingly aroused. She almost seemed to be enjoying it; it was extremely sexual, their voices growing louder and louder, and Maria eventually reached a kind of climax, gasping 'Stop! Stop! You're killing him!'

He proceeded to go to work on the other two. Each was different, one claiming to have eight devils inside her, 'and they're having babies!', but both, like Maria, appeared to enjoy the experience and when it was over all three asked for more. While the nun was being danced on I tried surreptitiously to take my camera from my bag, but before I could take a picture the priest abruptly ordered me to put it away. So all I could do was watch, terrified that at any moment I'd hear a rib snap or the crunch of a pubic bone, trying to remember all the details so that later I would be able to inform someone with the authority to stop it. The damage this man was doing both mentally and physically to the three girls, and God knows how many more from the past, was terrifying to contemplate. I hardly slept a wink all night as I lay with the others, lined up on the floor beneath the bed, thinking of how I had been directed there by the villagers, how the priest had done nothing to hide the presence of the girls from the wedding guests – perhaps everyone knew what was going on?

My enquiries after I'd left the next morning proved this to be true – all those I asked confirmed that the priest was well known and respected for his healing powers. When I told them about the dancing and the shrieking, they merely shrugged – if that was the way to rid a possessed soul of the devil, then so be it; the man should know, he's a priest after all. I wondered how much of this went on all over the country – and if it was so recognized, what could I do about it? I decided to wait until I reached the orphanage at Yonashen when I could talk to others about what to do, and I tried not to feel so disturbed – after all, I had come looking for strange local customs.

SECTION II

Yonashen

Chapter 4

Food, Glorious Food

The final day's walk to Yonashen seemed to take forever. I stuck to the main road for the shortest route but there were few trees and the sun beat down without mercy. I was tired after my sleepless night at the priest's house, but the traffic meant I had to walk the whole way and couldn't take a ride in the cart.

The countryside was different on this eastern side of the River Suchava. The mountains and forests had almost completely disappeared and I was in much more open country, with large ploughed fields and sweeping acres of maize plantations. For the first time I saw hay in bales rather than hand-made stacks, and I recognized the huge tractors and regimented buildings of collective farms. I had come across these before in the larger valleys, but here it seemed that there were no privately owned small plots at all. The roads were straight and boring, and I instinctively disliked the area.

I knew I must be close when some men passed by wearing sweatshirts emblazoned with '*The Sunday and Daily Telegraph: Quality Reading Seven Days a Week*' – British aid supplies couldn't be far away. Two women came up to me asking for medicine, very different from the usual presumption that I was a Russian and the enquiries as to what I had for sale.

My map showed that the village of Yonashen was about

a mile up a track from the large *communa* of Virfu Cimpului, but I was still on the main road when I saw a most welcome sight – the Land Rover! Unfortunately it was not in action, however; it was parked in someone's gateway with the bonnet up and two men were delving into its innards as I hailed a welcome. Their faces were highly amusing as I saw them take in the donkey and cart, with realization suddenly dawning – 'So you're the Donkey Woman!'

They then looked rather shamefaced and began apologizing that I should find my vehicle in a state of disrepair, promising that it would soon be going again. The thought of spending months wandering about the country by cart and then turning up at Yonashen unannounced and throwing a wobbly because I couldn't use my Land Rover struck me as farcical and I began to laugh.

Both men seemed surprised that I was young and apparently fairly normal. They had all had an image, they said, of the 'Donkey Woman' as an eccentric old spinster. I realized that they weren't quite what I expected, either; I thought I'd find a band of self-righteous do-gooders, but these two didn't fit the mould at all. The younger one, Jon, was a geology graduate from Warwickshire, rather shy but very friendly, and he was being teased mercilessly about his stutter by Mike, a great big man with an equally huge laugh who had just driven out from England with an articulated lorry-load of loos, showers and plumbing equipment. This was his sixth trip, he said; he had a haulage company back home, fast being driven to bankruptcy by him spending all the profits and more on bringing supplies out to Romania. He seemed very cheerful about the impending doom, though, saying, 'I love it out here, you see, so what can I do?'

Temporary lodging for me was quickly arranged; I could stay with the family in whose yard we were currently standing with the Land Rover. Hannibal could be tethered next door in Moona's garden until something more permanent was arranged. Moona Wolfe Murray was the man I had heard about back home, the one who had started the whole volunteer presence at Yonashen – but, Jon and Mike told me, he was away at the moment trying to raise some money in Italy.

A girl called Fiona then arrived in a van, looking much smarter than her vehicle, having been at a meeting with local government officials at the town hall in Botoshani, twenty miles away. She introduced herself as the volunteer doctor at Yonashen. She too was hardly what I expected, as she invited me into the house for a coffee, quickly changed into jeans and a T-shirt, and regaled me with stories of her attempts the previous day to introduce some of the children to her two kittens. One had almost been strangled and the other was still too terrified by the experience to venture from his box.

I was desperate to go and see the orphanage, which for some reason astonished Jon and Mike.

'But aren't you tired?' they asked. 'Aren't you hungry?' They seemed to think I'd need at least a couple of days' rest to prepare me for what lay at the top of the hill. I was now feeling wide awake and excited, however, and as soon as they'd produced a spark of life from the Land Rover I persuaded them to down their tools.

We followed a steep, rough track through fields of wheat and thistles to a long ridge, beyond which stretched a huge forest as far as the eye could see. The track turned right along the top of the ridge and after about two hundred yards we entered a small village, made up of the type of small peasant dwellings that I had seen all over Romania. Beyond the houses I spotted a large, noble-man's dwelling, rising high above a six-foot concrete wall surrounding it. A tower dominated the nearest end, rising from a long wing that led from an elaborately-columned entrance. We drove up to rickety iron gates constituting the shabby entrance. Nailed to a small gatehouse at the right hand side was a rotting wooden board proclaiming the nature of the establishment – CAMIN SPITAL PENTRU COPII HANDICAPAT SEVER SI IRECUPERABIL (Residential Hospital for Severely and Irrecuperably Handicapped Children).

A man appeared from the gatehouse and the gates were opened. We drove through and I saw a long building with a very grand pillared entrance. The central two-storey part of the house had a tower rising up to its left and a short wing built out to the front. To the right a long wing stretched off towards a large, three-storey tower, and another block had been built on to the back of this.

The general air was one of extreme scruffiness. Off-white paint was peeling from the outside walls and some of the windows were broken. Outside the right-hand wing was a Portakabin, and beyond this were two forty foot cargo containers. Piles of wood and bricks lay everywhere, and to the left of the gate lay great mounds of scrap and rubbish.

As soon as we drove through the gates I understood why Jon and Mike had suggested I rest before venturing in here. We were immediately surrounded by dozens of shouting children. They opened my door for me and dragged me out, hugging on to me and jumping up to give me great slobbery kisses. We'd only just parked the Land Rover when someone let the air out of one of the tyres, arousing a desperate yell from Jon as he chased the culprit over to the far side of the compound. Mike helped me fight a path towards the building. We took a left up the stone staircase from the hall and rushed into a room at the top, Mike quickly slamming shut and bolting the door behind us.

I looked around at a large messy room full of Western looking people and suddenly felt more overwhelmed than I had by the children. It was two months since I'd last spoken a word of English; it had been okay with Jon and Mike, but suddenly I felt an outsider, frightened by all these people who knew each other, chatting in strong Scottish and Irish accents. It was as if I'd forgotten how to communicate to people of my own age and culture, and I felt awkward and stupid. I was introduced to names that I instantly forgot and I couldn't think of anything to say to them. There was mail waiting for me and I buried myself in that instead, wishing I could join in the animated conversations going on around me.

A very efficient looking nurse in her early thirties called Alison offered to take me on a tour of the building. First she gave me a quick run-down of the place. There were 118 children at Yonashen, ranging in age from three to twenty-one. They had all been classed by Romanian doctors as having an IQ of under 25 and were therefore regarded as 'irrecuperable'. An IQ of under 25 would render someone as little more than a vegetable, yet I could hear some of these children speaking in English. There must be something very wrong with the doctors, I thought. Alison then told me that the test is carried out at the baby orphanages when the children are three years old. It is based on achievements such as toilet training, counting and the quality of their spoken language; many of them, however, had been institutionalized since birth and had never received any form of individual attention from which to learn such skills. Therefore the true range of abilities at Yonashen is enormous. There are deaf children, blind children, children with speech defects. There are some with cerebral palsy and one with muscular dystrophy. But the 'irrecuperable handicap' of the majority is not a classifiable mental or physical disability but severe emotional disturbance. Most were probably born normal and healthy. It was the experience of total neglect and deprivation that has caused such damage to their minds – handicap by nurture rather than nature.

Alison told me that the orphanage was divided into

three sections which the volunteers called by the Romanian names used by the staff and children. '*Copii Mici*', for small children from the age of roughly three to six, was situated in three rooms at the top of the large tower at the northern end of the building. '*In Fatsa*', the rooms leading off the long, wide corridor that led along the front of the building to the right of the main entrance, was where the more capable older children lived. At the back, in a wing of its own, was '*Triaj*', the section reserved for the most seriously disturbed children. The rooms throughout had the cold dark stamp of 'institution' all over them. The floors were of grey stone, the ceilings were high, the windows small and barred. The walls had been brightly painted with animals and cartoon characters, but damp was creeping through in many places and it was evidently a constant battle to stop the paint from flaking off.

As we set off down the long front corridor of the *In Fatsa* section, there was an air of unbelievable chaos, a sea of arms grabbing at me and little faces looking up expectantly. No newspaper article or photograph could ever have prepared me for the reality of actually meeting these children. Maybe it was the effect of having every sense bombarded at once – it was the smell, that strange combination of damp walls, fresh paint, human filth, bleach and God knows what else, that lingers in some of my clothes to this day. It was the way they reached out to touch me, to kiss me, to grab at my hands, so that I didn't know which direction to turn. It was the way they stared into my eyes; they were no longer simply a poignant image of neglect, but very real individuals with needs and feelings that were entirely here and now. It was the noise, the shouting and the banging and the shrieks.

They all had shaved heads and it was difficult not to think of them all as boys. They were wearing extraordinary assortments of clothes, some with their trousers down by their ankles, others wearing endless layers of jumpers despite the heat of the afternoon. The rooms were crammed full of bunks and, apart from a tiny play area in the tower for the small children, there were no dayrooms or classrooms. One of the windows was smashed just as we'd walked past it, a boy having hurled a stone at it. He ran up to grab a jagged piece of glass, jubilantly making off with his new weapon.

The stench of human excrement told me we must be nearing the toilet facilities, but as I put my head round the doorway and tried not to breathe through my nose I was surprised to see five grown men in there, hacking at the walls and measuring the floor. I was introduced to the plumbers, recently arrived from England alongside Mike's truckful of equipment which they were about to install. I gaped at the holes in the floor that served as loos and the single cold shower that up till then had been the only facility for cleaning the children, and I heard how over the next fortnight they were going to install flushing upright toilets, hot water showers and rows of sinks. I couldn't quite picture it and could say little more than 'Wow!', once again despairing of my current inability to communicate in my own language.

We moved on to the section for the most disturbed children – *Triaj* – and found complete pandemonium. Jackie and Emma, two young English volunteer nurses, were trying to make sure all the children had clean nappies on before they could escape to the volunteer room at the end of a long day. Their efforts, however, were being seriously hampered by one of the larger girls who kept grabbing the dirty nappies from the bin and putting them back on the smaller children. I would have laughed if my hair wasn't being pulled quite so hard by a little fair-haired boy who looked the spitting image of Damien from *The Omen* and was staring at me as if intent to kill. Other children were sitting quietly on their bunks, banging their heads against the walls, staring intently at their hands, clearly in far-away worlds of their own. A little dark-haired boy was urinating on one of the mattresses; a girl was busy at a window dismantling mosquito netting.

Meanwhile I noticed three Romanian women in blue overalls standing at the doorway watching, arms folded, with expressions of amused boredom. They were the care workers, Jackie said matter of factly, and I guessed from her tone of voice that their not lifting a finger to help was nothing out of the ordinary.

I escaped up a winding stone stairway to the tower and the younger children's section. I couldn't believe that the children were all over three and some as old as eight. The inhabitants of the rows and rows of cots crammed from corner to corner looked like babies – I would hardly have guessed that any of them were over two. These were the huggable, adorable faces of all those documentaries about Romanian orphans we'd been bombarded with back home. As I picked them up and played with them their eyes lit up and they gurgled and laughed, while their neighbour in the next cot looked on, silently waiting his turn. There were about twenty children in each small room; compared to the *Triaj* and Front Corridor (*In Fatsa*) children they were all unbelievably cute and appealing. This was what I had imagined it would be like, I think – just a sea of adorable faces, tugging at the heartstrings. It was extremely difficult to leave, every maternal instinct in my body aroused.

The Front Corridor children were the ones who had rushed out to greet us on my arrival. They were older; there were about forty of them apparently, but it didn't seem as crowded as the other sections because they were free to wander about the whole building and grounds. Many seemed to have nothing wrong with them at all. They bombarded me with questions, asking what my name was, if I'd be staying for long, whether I could get them a drink of water. Again, their sizes astonished me; all were over seven apparently, but some I would have put at no more than three. They were incredibly active; a new face was apparently cause for great joy, and they screeched at deafening pitches to be heard above everyone else.

It was their supper time and I followed them to the dining hall in the far wing of the building. It was a relatively large room filled with two long rows of tables and benches alongside. The meal itself was anarchy in action. Blue-overalled staff gave out bowls of white slop and hunks of bread which the children were eating as quickly as possible with the aim of then grabbing their neighbour's bowl before he had finished, resulting in tears and scuffles while the staff tried to intervene with cuffs round the ear. There were some spoons about but most tipped the bowls straight into their mouths or scooped with their hands. I sat down amongst them and was soon covered in food as five children fought for my lap space, simultaneously making grabs at each other's bowls.

I escaped to the back and tried to talk to the women with the pots and ladles, enquiring after the nature of the food they had just served. They merely shrugged, however, saying that it was '*strain*' – foreign. I looked bemused and they helped me out with that magical word '*ajutoare*' – aid. I tasted the stuff myself but apart from a distinct flavour of milk powder I still couldn't tell what it was meant to be. I asked if I could see the packet and was taken round the back to the kitchen, a pleasantly large room dominated by a large oil-fired oven in the centre. I was presented with a formidable collection of empty tins and boxes and I discovered that the ingredients for the extraordinary mixture had been instant mashed potato, porridge oats, dried mixed vegetable soup and baby food cereal, plus the powdered milk that I had already identified.

I retired upstairs to the volunteers' room and sat feeling rather dazed, listening to the chatter around me. Talk centred on a fence being put up around an adventure playground at the back of the building. A very tall, gangly man called Henry, with a barely comprehensible Scottish accent which he combined with his own version of Romanian, was introduced as resident artist at Yonashen. He was responsible for many of the brilliant murals in the orphanage, and was stamping round the room fuming that the director had stopped him from finishing his 'Thomas the Tank Engine'. Further enquiry revealed this to be a huge oil drum in the garden, a rusty eyesore that Henry had started transforming with paint. The reason for such killjoy behaviour was not known, but the curses flying around suggested that relations with the director – called Mitica – were not always smooth.

'Mitica's all right, really,' I was told, especially when compared with what they'd had to cope with before. A young Scottish girl called Susan whom I'd seen upstairs working in the small children's section in the tower (*Copii Mici*), proceeded to regale me with stories of the boss under whom Yonashen had suffered up until March. She was a woman referred to as 'Doamna Jetta', which was spoken in the way a Dalmatian might spit out the name Cruella deVille. She had apparently hampered their every move, demanding bribes before allowing them to make any changes at all. On the anniversary of the revolution the previous December, police had arrived at Yonashen to arrest the volunteers for the 'crime of stealing their own aid'. It was the result of complaints that volunteers had made about missing supplies, before they discovered that Doamna Jetta had extremely good friends in the police force. Moona Wolfe Murray had finally succeeded in getting her replaced by the current director, Mitica, who was well-intentioned and honest, if out of his depth and intimidated by the volunteer presence. He appeared to be trying to resolve the latter problem by embarking on a power struggle to show just who was in charge – hence Henry was not being allowed to create his 'Thomas the Tank Engine' because he had not asked Mitica's permission first.

I drove back down the track and was deposited with my assigned family, with whom I found conversation much easier than I had with my fellow volunteers. The family turned out to be extremely nice – a middle-aged couple called Mihai and Amalia and their five children. They had a large house by Romanian standards; this one had four rooms rather than the usual two. One was the kitchen with the stove and next to this was the room where the whole family slept. At the other side of the house were two smart rooms which, before the arrival of foreigners in the village, they would have used only rarely to entertain at special occasions. Now, however, one room was kept for the use of Rupert Wolfe Murray, Moona's brother, when he came out to Yonashen, and I was given the other, larger, one. It had been beautifully decorated, the walls covered with pictures including a painted photograph of Amalia looking stunning as a young woman.

It was evident that Mihai and Amalia were used to foreigners staying in their home, for they were happy to let me come and go as I pleased. They left me alone when I went to my room, something that would never happen in a normal Romanian household. Over the next few days I spent most of my free time with them, feeling much more comfortable in their familiar culture than in the one that was meant to be my own.

The next morning, I joined the others in the volunteers' room for the 8.30 daily meeting to sort out work to be done and problems to solve. It was presided over by Fiona, the doctor, in Moona's absence, but it was an informal affair. People were making tea, grabbing something to eat, and there were continual interruptions as stories were told and suggestions made.

I gained a better idea of what everyone actually did all day. There were over twenty volunteers working at Yonashen at that time; most were involved in the day-to-day care of the children, working in shifts so as to be in the sections for almost all their charges' waking hours. Talk centred on lack of nappies in *Triaj* and a new Portakabin that had just arrived and was being transformed into a schoolroom for the older Front Section children. A pretty, dark-haired girl called Collette, whom I'd noticed arrive in the volunteers' room the previous evening looking wan and exhausted, was asked if she could survive continuing her work down in the laundry. She laughed and said she thought she'd last a little while longer. Two girls were given a painting assignment that was expected to last a week or so, and Henry took some specifications for shelves. Issy, a tall, thin woman with long red hair, spoke to all of us about an 'Incident Book' that she was leaving in the volunteers' room. In it she wanted all cases of staff misconduct to be reported and signed by the witness, which sounded ominous.

Everybody seemed well-organized and rushed off as soon as the meeting was over, leaving me feeling rather stupid and terrified of getting in the way. Fiona asked me to join her in a small office along the corridor and we discussed ways in which I could be put to use during my stay.

Fiona was instantly likeable although quiet and reserved compared to many of the other volunteers. She was quite tall with short dark hair and large brown eyes in a pretty face. She seemed far too young to have the responsibility for Yonashen upon her shoulders, and she gave the impression of it weighing down heavily at times. Her affection for the children shone through whenever she mentioned them; while we talked we were disturbed by three boisterous intruders and I was impressed by their evident love for her.

During our talk I found it hard to come up with anything more constructive than 'I'll do anything', but I was aware that my greatest asset was my ability to speak Romanian and the fact that with my Land Rover I had transport. Fiona suggested I carry out a food survey;

she wanted to know exactly to what extent the children's nutritional requirements were being met, and how much the orphanage was relying on donated foreign food. After my experience of the children's supper the night before, I reckoned this would be interesting, to say the least.

I was taken down to the kitchen and introduced to the cooking staff. I instantly felt like a spy, however, and soon gave up questioning them, deciding it was more important to gain their trust first. Thus I ended up spending most of that first day just talking, discussing safe topics and telling them about my travels. There was a hook-nosed woman called Lenutsa who seemed to be in charge of the storeroom, which was a well-padlocked place around the back. She was most unwilling to let me see this, and for the moment I didn't push the subject. A large friendly man called Ili was doing most of the cooking, putting chunks of pork fat and vegetables into a large cauldron, and two other women were peeling potatoes and washing pans.

Ili kept himself to himself and didn't open up to me much, but the other women were only too pleased to have an excuse to chat. They told me of their children, of their meagre wages, of the general misery of their lives, and I soon felt fed up with them – not one mentioned anything about the orphanage children. I realize now that I had grown harsh since the start of my travels, but these women's lives were no different from that of any other ordinary Romanian and their moaning only struck me as selfish. They did not appear to regard the orphanage children as being worthy of any sympathy at all.

However, I listened and I smiled, and my patience was rewarded by my coming away at the end of the day with a month's worth of official menu forms. Each day Lenutsa had to fill in a piece of paper listing the exact ingredients used, the prices of each, and the names of the meals that were concocted out of them. The list was checked and approved by the orphanage administrator, a man called

Radu who seemed to be continually wandering around the building and grounds looking shifty. The list was then sent to the accounts department in a room upstairs which I didn't yet dare venture into. I could hardly believe my luck, for I'd imagined that I'd have to hang around for hours in the kitchen, weighing everything out and generally making a nuisance of myself while Ili tried to cook.

I returned victorious to the volunteers' room, but then spent the rest of the week crouched over a magnifying glass, a calculator and a dictionary as I tried to work out the indecipherable handwriting of the carbon copies I'd been given. Lenutsa wasn't much help; she said I couldn't see the originals once they'd been sent to accounts, and her eyesight was poor, so even though she had written them in the first place, she was no better than I was at understanding the list. Her guesses as to what she'd taken from the store a month ago were wildly inaccurate.

I discovered that the children ate no green vegetables and no fresh fruit (except for an orange each that they'd been given from an aid truck on 12 May). They were given no fresh milk, no eggs, no cheese, no fish other than tinned sardines, and no white meat. When I looked in the fridges I discovered that most of the 'meat' written on the menu lists consisted of little but bones and pork fat. As I went through it all I found myself growing increasingly angry. I knew that the markets had been full of fresh locally-grown vegetables since May, all of it costing less than five pence a pound. Most of the aid food they were using, listed separately, consisted of items that I knew were relatively plentiful within Romania and could have been bought for a fraction of the prices that they would have cost at home.

I grew less worried about offending the kitchen staff and began asking questions. Why did they not use fresh pro-duce? Why did they say they needed foreign baked beans when they could be bought in the shop down the road? Why did they spend more on biscuits than on meat?

To each enquiry I was given a selection of three answers: 'we don't have enough money'; 'it's impossible to buy fresh produce'; and 'foreign food tastes so much nicer, the children like it so much more'. I tried to talk about nutrition, about protein and vitamins and a well-balanced diet, but was faced with entirely blank expressions. I discovered that they thought entirely in terms of calories. Hence pork fat is a much more sensible food than chicken, and biscuits are better than apples. Powdered milk is better than fresh since it is more concentrated, and because it is Western it must be of higher quality than the stuff that comes out of Romanian cows. Again and again I met the presumption that anything Western must be marvellous, be it a vitamin tablet or a Safeway's teabag. I began to realize that my 'food survey' could turn into a very great task indeed if I wanted to make any kind of changes.

I spoke to Fiona about the effect of the children's diet on their health; I was surprised that they weren't thinner – some were actually fat – but Fiona told me that this is deceptive. Even some of the podgy ones were apparently suffering from classical malnutrition symptoms such as rickets and skin disease. The endless supply of stodge in bread and potatoes, the fatty stew and sugary tea, meant their calorific intake was often higher than it should have been, but they weren't getting the vitamins and proteins to put those calories to good use.

I began investigating the kitchen staff's complaints – namely that they didn't have enough money. Once again I ploughed through all the ingredient listings, this time checking the prices. The daily food allowance from the Romanian Government was 76 *lei* per child, which multiplied by 118 gave a quota for Yonashen of 8,968 *lei* a day – about 25 pounds, which as a total for feeding 118 children seemed very little and I began to sympathize with the staff. As I worked through the lists, however, I thought that I must be making a mistake, that perhaps I should be including the price of fuel for the oven or wages for the kitchen staff. But investigation revealed that no, the allowance was purely for the food itself. I checked and rechecked the figures, but found that during the previous month the most that had been spent on food in any one day was 5,900 *lei*; the average was about 4,000 and on some days it was as little as 2,000 *lei*. Alarm bells began ringing in my head.

I tried to speak to Lenutsa about the deficiency but all she would tell me was that Doamna Jetta was in charge of the money.

'But I thought Doamna Jetta was the woman who had been the boss here up until March?'

'That's right, and now she's head of accounts.'

The plot was thickening and I didn't know what to do. Apparently it had not been possible to actually get Doamna Jetta sacked the previous March; instead she had just been demoted. It had been hoped that she wouldn't be able to do too much damage in accounts due to the fact that Mitica, the new director, loathed her. She was universally hated by the volunteers. She was a fat, ugly woman of about fifty-five: she never smiled and her small beady eyes shone out with her hatred of us. She now presided over the accounts room next to Mitica's office. She became irate if a volunteer set foot in there, physically pushing them back out of the door with much screeching. I told other volunteers of what I had found and the general suggestion was that I should tell Mitica who probably didn't have a clue about what was happening and would want to know.

Mitica was a small, pasty-faced man without a neck. He had light brown hair and bright eyes that made him look very nice when he smiled. He was usually to be found in a total fluster about some minor disaster such as the phone lines not working, or his lack of a lift home to Botoshani in the evening. I liked him even though he drove me mad on occasions; despite his frequent outbursts against the volunteers, you could tell that his heart was in the right place.

At this stage, just a week since my arrival, I had only spoken to him a few times. He obviously didn't approve of what I was doing; he had made it clear that volunteers were meant to be here to work, not to snoop around the kitchen with calculators. So I had tried to keep out of his way, and felt ridiculously nervous as I knocked on his office door. He was most polite, however, inviting me in and listening to what I had to say without interruption. I showed him the lists of figures and as he went through them I saw his face grow tense with anger. He rushed to the door and yelled a series of orders into the corridor, demanding to see Lenutsa and Ili, Doamna Jetta and Radu. Slowly they gathered, and I tried to disappear into my chair as Mitica demanded an explanation for the figures. Four pairs of eyes shot daggers at me and I wondered whether I'd ever be able to set foot in the kitchen again after such treachery.

Their excuses revived my anger. Their central argument was that it involved far too much effort to change the menus after the quota went up from 45 *lei* to 76 *lei* in April; and anyway, with inflation running so high, the shop prices were bound to go up soon and it would be cruel to accustom the children to better food if it would only have to be cut back again. I volunteered the suggestion that perhaps the money could have been spent on buying in supplies before the expected price rises occurred, to which Mitica in turn suggested that I might like to leave the room. I could hear raised voices for the next twenty minutes, and was satisfied that if there was a conspiracy Mitica at least was not part of it.

I returned to see him later in the day and he thanked me, but when I enquired about what he planned to do about the problem, he told me that he had simply ordered them to spend more money on food. I began asking where the missing money could be, but was abruptly told that was no business of mine. An attempt to suggest what the extra money should be spent on resulted in a withering look clearly meaning 'Don't you dare tell me how to do my job' and I withdrew, realizing I'd caused enough trouble for one day.

The next morning, my apprehensions about facing the kitchen staff ended up as a ridiculously boisterous entrance through the dining-room door. I burst forth with suggestions and huge enthusiastic smiles about how we could spend the extra money on milk and eggs and vegetables, almost as if I'd just effected a huge increase for them in the amount they were allowed to go out and spend. They seemed happy to go along with this interpretation of events but managed to come up with negative replies to all my ideas, mainly in the form of it being impossible to purchase such food in the nearby town of Buchecha; it could only be found in Botoshani, the capital of the county twenty miles away, and with only a horse and cart as transport such journeys were not possible.

'But what about having it delivered? There's a dairy farm down the road, surely we could buy milk direct from there? Villagers grow vegetables, couldn't we buy their surplus?'

Ili smiled and shook his head in amusement, while Lenutsa just looked at me as if I'd gone mad. She told me, very slowly as if explaining to someone of very low intelligence, that the food had to be bought from the state shop in Buchecha, that you couldn't buy all the stuff I was talking about from there, and you weren't allowed to buy from private traders. I replied equally slowly that I didn't know whether they had heard, but there had been a revolution recently and you were allowed to spend your money as you saw fit. I then learnt that they couldn't buy anything with cash; payment was through Government cheques, which were only accepted by state-owned shops. I didn't have a convenient answer to that one and was forced to retire with a Schwarzenegger-style 'I'll be back'.

I was determined to prove them all wrong and thus began a systematic investigation into Romanian food retailing. It started at the farm at the bottom of the village, a huge collective of regimented barns and heaps of broken machinery. I had already met the vet who seemed to be in charge of the place when I was hunting for a blacksmith for Hannibal. He was a nice old man in the best Communist tradition and, unasked, had given me at least a month's supply of hay and corn for Hannibal, refusing to accept a single *lei* for them. He was now fascinated by my desire to supply the orphanage with fresh milk and said that, yes, they did have dairy cows on the farm. But there was a major problem – like most other collectives in this part of Romania, they had many TB-carrying cows. Therefore the milk had to be sent into the pasteurization plant in Botoshani before it could be sold.

I asked about the cows owned privately by the villagers, for I'd learnt that their surplus milk was currently being bought by the farm so as to make up the latter's quota. There was apparently no guarantee against their having TB either. I thought of all the milk I had drunk on my travels, often straight from the cow, and realized that the unimmunized children could not be put at such risk. So the only option left was to organize a way of delivering pasteurized milk to Yonashen from Botoshani.

I tried to keep away from the kitchen staff, since all their 'I told you so's' were becoming depressing. No Romanian seemed remotely interested in helping me think of a solution. Mitica told me it was all far too complicated to be practical. 'And anyway,' he said, 'we can get foreign aid supplies of powdered milk, so what are you worried about?' The notion that the aid trucks might one day stop coming was apparently something not to be contemplated. It was left to me to work out a solution, which had I been Romanian and understood the system would have come to me in a matter of minutes, but since I wasn't and didn't, it took many weeks of trial and error, of depressed gloom and excited brain-waves.

Chapter 5

Falling for the Kids

Meanwhile I grew used to life at Yonashen and began to feel at home. Moona Wolfe Murray returned from Italy and I was introduced to one of the most charismatic men I have ever had the good fortune to work with. Moona was adored by the children and admired by almost every Romanian in the area. He had dark, almost black hair, bright blue eyes and was always gesticulating frantically when he spoke. With a very animated face, he had the air of a naughty twelve-year-old, was permanently dishevelled in his dress, was often frustratingly disorganized, and spoke Romanian with a hilariously strong Scottish accent. Yet more and more I found myself trying to ape his methods, for he quite literally charmed the pants off everyone he met. Entirely unpretentious, he dealt with Romanian officials by offering up a seemingly endless supply of good humour. He worked on the principle that if you can make them like you, they will help you: he turned his youth and naïvety to his advantage, always asking their advice and building up their self-importance so that he never came across as a pompous Westerner instructing them on how to run their affairs – a trap that I had already found myself falling into. The Moona Charm School was the best training possible for achieving results; as well as that I liked him. For the first time I found I could talk about my travels and feelings for the country with someone whose enthusiasm for Romanian culture far surpassed my own. His optimism for what could be achieved at Yonashen was endless and he was constantly coming up with new ideas for ways in which the children and the community as a whole could be helped.

Gradually I grew to know more of the children. Because I wasn't actually working in the sections, the children I had most contact with were the most capable ones from the Front Section. They were outside most of the day amusing themselves, and their boredom I could help to alleviate by taking them for rides in the Land Rover when I went into town, or by bringing them home with me for dog walks and donkey rides, a home-cooked meal and a glimpse of village life. There was Silvio, a beautiful little boy of about eight. By Yonashen standards Silvio was polite and well-mannered. He would never hurt you to get attention, and he would enjoy a quiet one-to-one conversation. He was terrified of the dogs but would throw Herculean tantrums if he knew he was missing out on a walk.

There was Nicolae, a desperately clingy and affectionate child who smiled at everyone, whether they were being kind to him or hitting him. He had brown hair and dark skin, and enormous sticking-out ears which made him look very endearing. He did very badly in the dog-eat-dog atmosphere of Yonashen, for though he was one of the more capable ones, he was useless at fending for himself and fighting for a place at the top of the pile. He latched on to me immediately and would follow me round pathetically. He adored the dogs and going for walks was the highlight of his day. His speech was very difficult to understand, coming out in frantic stuttering outbursts, and he insisted on calling me '*Shosea*', a Romanian word meaning main road.

Mushat was a highly capable boy in his late teens who had managed to pick up an incredible amount of English – expressions which he delivered in exact mimicry of the Scottish and Irish accents of the volunteers. I even mistook him for a volunteer when he first greeted me with 'Hey, man, whatcha doin'?' Depending on his mood he could be helpful with the younger ones and jobs around the orphanage, and could be trusted to relay information – he was one of the very few bilingual people at Yonashen. At other times, however, he caused havoc with his deviously cunning lies. Unfortunately Mushat was much too much hard work to be able to take into town very often. In meetings he would join in and begin arguing with the bigwig from whom I was trying to cajole a favour, but if I left him outside in the car he would wander off on shop-lifting sprees.

From my past experience of children I knew of their amazing ability to pick up the words and expressions that adults least want them to understand. This proved to be especially true of the English learnt by the orphans of Yonashen. They soon realized the excellent shock factor to be had from repeating those words uttered by volunteers at moments of extreme duress and, once learnt, it proved impossible to convince them not to use such language at the most inopportune moments. The worst culprit was a boy named Cezar, who was actually sixteen but due to a growth hormone deficiency looked a very cute eight. He had blue eyes, golden curly hair and would adopt a cherubic expression as he poured forth expletives worthy of a depraved Borstal inmate. This proved highly embarrassing when we had visits from Western charity groups, come to see whether we were worthy of their donations.

'Aah, what a sweet little boy! Come and sit on my lap – would you like to play?'

'Fuck off, you smelly fat shithead!' would come the reply, leaving us in cringing embarrassment as the highly offended Westerner inquired as to who had taught the child such language. We practically had to lock him up when religious groups came round, so great was his ability to cause sudden withdrawals of offers of financial assistance.

Slowly I developed friendships with the other volunteers, often being called in to translate between those working in the sections and the Romanian staff that they were trying to influence. The official position of the volunteers at Yonashen was to be there as the invited guests of the Romanian management, to give support and advice to the Romanian staff and financial help in the provision of supplies. In reality this usually meant that the local peasant women on the payroll sat back and watched while the volunteers did most of the work. There were some notable exceptions, of course, especially in the younger ones employed since foreigners had arrived; but on the whole it was extremely difficult to influence the older women, who for years had controlled the children with canes and whose Victorian attitudes meant they regarded a handicapped child as little more than an animal. Corporal punishment was the norm, even for a very young child who could hardly walk, and since we had no authority over the Romanian staff we were relatively powerless to stop it. All we could do if we witnessed violence was report it in Issy's incident book and show it to Mitica, in the hope that he might discipline the staff member involved. I happened to be in his office when such a disciplinary action was taking place, in the early days before he realized how good my Romanian was. I heard him give the obligatory warning; however, it was followed by a much more severe reprimand that the woman had been stupid enough to let a foreigner see her doing it.

One day about a week after my arrival two volunteers – Emma, who worked in *Triaj*, and Collette, the laundry slave – were leaving the orphanage late in the evening. They had walked just beyond the gate when they heard screams coming from within the building; they rushed back to find one of the Front Section children, a deaf boy of about twelve known as 'Blondu', being severely beaten by one of the staff. They rescued him and were so shocked by what they had seen that they ended up staying in the orphanage all night in case anything else happened.

I heard all this reported at the morning meeting the next day, after which I was meant to be taking Emma and Collette in the Land Rover to go and find the owner of a house that they wanted to rent. They suggested bringing Blondu with us to give him a treat, and thus I was introduced to a funny-looking child with white hair, huge sticking-out ears and a big grin. He clambered in beside me and watched fascinated at the controls as we set off, leaning down to see what my feet were doing and pressing the horn for me whenever we overtook a horse and cart. When Emma passed round her cigarettes he grabbed the lighter from her, holding it out to each of us like a perfect little gentleman.

The search for the landlady turned into something of a wild goose chase, for we were told that she was out working in the fields and we ended up shifting into four-wheel drive and clambering through ditches as we drove from cluster to cluster of peasants hoeing their tiny far-flung plots of newly-allocated land. Blondu found the whole expedition hilarious, screaming with laughter whenever we got stuck, and I found myself growing fascinated by this little boy who was deaf and dumb yet somehow managed to be always communicating.

It was to be the start of a special relationship. Just as I found him fascinating, Blondu seemed to think that a girl with a Land Rover was well worth knowing. As I began my missions to the county's various food retailers, I soon discovered that I had double the success rate if a skinny little waif was at my side doing a heartrending impression of Oliver Twist. We perfected our act to a T; Blondu would be good as gold, confining his activities to lighting cigarettes and, at a nod from me, looking up appealingly through thick lashes at the most important moments of my appeals for assistance.

I'm still not sure if he had any idea of what we were actually doing. Fiona was trying to introduce the teaching of Maketon, a type of sign language, but Blondu and some of the other children at Yonashen had long used a primitive self-invented sign language of their own amongst themselves. My own knowledge of Maketon was confined to the hand from chin gesture meaning thank you, and a thumbs up sign for anything good. Other than that, Blondu and I got by with an enthusiastic mixture of facial expressions and exaggerated movements. Somehow we managed to have quite detailed conversations, and I was aware of the emotional bonds between us developing frighteningly quickly.

I began taking him on dog walks. He was completely unfazed by William's size and appearance and treated both dogs as his own from the start. For the duration of the walk he would ignore me and the other children with us and run off alone with the dogs, giving out commands through a series of whistles and gestures which suggested he'd spent his life training collies on the fells. Blondu was also something of an acrobat when it came to riding Hannibal. Most of the children I took home to ride in the cart or play on his back were understandably nervous, for Hannibal isn't the most docile of donkeys and I'd often have to grab his head as he tried to give a none too friendly nip or charge off at a gallop whenever he got bored. Blondu, however, was totally fearless. He didn't like me holding the leading rein and would canter off on his own, totally out of control but usually managing to stay on. He even succeeded in persuading Hannibal to jump – an extraordinary feat for any donkey, let alone one as notoriously stubborn and lazy as Hannibal. I began imagining that Blondu came from a circus family, or was perhaps descended from Hungarian horsemen in Transylvania.

Blondu's origins were a mystery. I discovered that he had no name and no papers; he was merely known as

'Blondu' because of the colour of his hair. He had been found by the police wandering the streets of Botoshani in 1986. They had brought him to Yonashen and no efforts had been made to find out who he was – being deaf and dumb he could hardly tell anyone. No one even knew his age; from his size he seemed to be about twelve, but at Yonashen guessing from size was often wildly inaccurate. The staff liked to think that he came from Russia, mainly because of his Slavic wide cheek-bones and very fair hair, but also because they vigorously maintained that it was impossible to 'lose' a child in Romania. Something about Blondu suggested that he had once enjoyed a normal mother–child relationship however, and I often wondered what had happened. If he'd been orphaned or abandoned at birth, like most of the children, I felt sure that he'd be a great deal more disturbed. Compared to most of the other children at Yonashen, Blondu was a very communicative little boy – doubly astonishing considering that he was deaf. The greatest problem with many was to bring them out of their own little worlds and teach them to be aware of their surroundings. Difficulties with Blondu concerned arguments about whether he would be allowed to have and do what he wanted, as with any normal child at home.

Not that he hadn't been affected by his experiences – he sometimes withdrew into a silent shell when he would go and hide, on top of a cupboard or up on the roof, curling himself into a ball and refusing to come down until he was ready. Or he would sit on my lap and for no apparent reason start silently sobbing, clinging on to me for dear life. He didn't often sleep at night and got up to various nocturnal antics that would sometimes land him in serious trouble with the staff and result in the kind of beatings that Emma and Collette had chanced to hear.

Blondu's speciality was roof climbing. He was as agile as a monkey and could climb along the window ledges and thin decorative bits of plaster on the orphanage walls, up on to the steep aluminium tiled roof with its turrets and towers. Usually he seemed to go up just for the freedom, but sometimes he was intent on more specific mischief and would break in through the upstairs windows into the directors' office, the medical cabinet or the volunteers' room. The latter became a favourite goal after the donation to the orphanage of a television and video. These were locked up at night for safekeeping, but Blondu worked out how to operate them and evidently spent many hours of amusement as he previewed the tapes that were shown supervised to larger audiences by day. Unfortunately he often managed to chew the tapes up in the process so he didn't endear himself to anyone by his ingenuity, and Fiona was frequently to be seen storming round the building trying to seek him out after discovering that her entire collection of plasters and bandages had disappeared from the medical room.

Things became more serious when the director found his office window smashed and papers scattered around the room. He was so furious that he organized for Blondu to have electric shock treatment at one of the hospitals in Botoshani. Apparently this would 'cure his mental problem', or at the very least teach him a lesson he wouldn't forget. Our outrage and refusal to co-operate with the plan luckily resulted in it being shelved, but we all had a feeling that Blondu was living on borrowed time. We began making more concerted efforts to keep him on ground level, barring all the upstairs windows and bringing him down from the roof whenever he was spotted up there. Another Irish girl called Colette (this time with short hair and spelling her name with a single 'l') shared Blondu's climbing abilities and was often to be seen clambering around after him while the rest of us watched in terror from below, sure that one or both would slip and come crashing forty feet to the concrete surrounding the building.

I also discovered that Blondu was something of an expert

at shop-lifting. When he came with me to the market I would give him some *lei* to buy something for himself. He immediately handed over the money to beggars and cripples on the street, usually introducing himself and shaking hands in the process, and then he proceeded to steal what he wanted from the stalls. It was the greatest source of contention between us, and he never forgave me for the time I caught him red-handed and put him through the humiliation of handing back a whistle and comb to the stallholder. What made it harder to explain the wrong of stealing was the fact that usually Blondu did not take things for himself. Often they were presents for *me*, for the staff, or for older boys in the hope that it would make them less likely to bully him. I was often presented with little gifts of cigarettes that I knew had once belonged to the gateman, and Blondu began making more and more elaborate key rings for the Land Rover. My favourite was a plastic donkey that he had attached to a bath plug chain, which I used for two weeks before I overheard someone in the volunteers' room complaining about their very expensive toy farm being rendered almost useless by so many of the parts having been stolen, presumably by Romanian staff. With a very red face I handed my donkey over, making feeble excuses about how I hadn't realized.

I was aware that I was growing too close to Blondu and that in the long run it wouldn't do either of us any good – when the time came for me to leave we were both going to be devastated. I began making a concerted effort to spread my affections more evenly, but in practice this didn't really work, the main result being that I became far too fond of two children instead of just one.

Blondu's best pal was a boy of about the same age called Florin. He was a beautiful child, with hazel eyes, light brown hair and flawless olive skin (it never ceased to amazed me that the teenagers at Yonashen, washing once a week when they were forced to, should have such beautiful complexions). We often used to argue about which film star Florin resembled, the usual choice being between Ian Charleson and Christopher Lambert from the film *Greystoke*. The latter was a somewhat strange coincidence due to the fact that Florin did not speak. Apart from '*da*' (yes) and '*nu*' (no), he point-blank refused to say a word.

I began to take Florin as well as Blondu to my meetings with Romanian officials. They were the only two children with whom it was always safe, due to the fact that they never spoke, so they didn't drop painfully embarrassing clangers at critical moments. The interaction between the two boys was incredible – with the subtlest of facial gestures they could communicate perfectly. Gradually I realized that Florin was remarkably intelligent. He understood everything I said in Romanian and he flabbergasted me by the amount of English he knew: a remark such as 'Damn, what have I done with my car keys?' would result in Florin quietly fetching them from the far side of the room. He was an incredibly responsible child; we should have created the position of Head Boy for him, or at least Orphanage Prefect. I could ask him to collect something from a store room, giving him the keys and trusting him implicitly not to let anyone else in there, not to steal anything, and to lock the door behind him. I could leave him in the Land Rover in town to guard the contents and know that he wouldn't wander off or start selling off the spare tyre and the windscreen wipers as most of the other children did. I could ask him to tell someone something and he would do his best in elaborate sign language; conversations with him were rather like the game where you have to find a person's assumed identity by asking questions that can only be answered by 'Yes' or 'No'.

Florin's refusal to speak was a great mystery. He had no physical speech impediment, as shown by the increasing number of English words that he used, but nothing would induce him to speak Romanian. Fiona could only think that it was an effect of the emotional trauma of being abandoned as a small child. Records revealed nothing save the fact that he had been admitted into care some time before the age of four, so there were endless possibilities of what may have happened to him – his mother may have died, he may have suffered abuse, he may have been very ill. Romanian medical opinion regarded him as severely mentally retarded, due to the fact that he refused to answer any of the questions in the verbal IQ tests used to determine ability.

Fiona had a plausible theory as to why he continued to refuse to speak Romanian. Due to his intelligence, Florin had considerable status at Yonashen amongst both the children and the staff; in the dog-eat-dog structure of the place he was fairly near the top. Many of the children did not talk and it was easy for him to survive without speech; in such an atmosphere he had much to lose by opening himself up to the ridicule that the learning and practice of speech would undoubtedly entail. If he pronounced a word wrong he would be laughed at by both the other kids and many of the care workers. With his English, however, he knew that we would not laugh at him. Fiona reckoned that as long as Florin stayed at Yonashen, he would probably never speak Romanian. If, however, he was brought out of that atmosphere and placed in a situation where he felt secure and safe from ridicule, and where he needed to speak Romanian to fit in, he would probably pick it up very quickly.

Meanwhile Florin and Blondu's lack of speech made them the easiest of companions as they joined me on my trips around the county, stopping me from becoming lonely or depressed after a frustrating day of fruitless encounters with uncompromising ex-Communists. We'd stop off at a restaurant on the way home and it was impossible not to feel happy as I watched them delightedly wolfing down double helpings of pork and chips. It was increasingly difficult to refuse their hopeful little faces that would always turn up whenever I got to within ten yards of the Land Rover; I tried to be fair and take other children when I could, but if I had much work to do it was useful to have Florin with me to keep them all in order, and Blondu would throw such tantrums if I refused to take him that it was usually easier just to say 'yes'.

My mission to improve the children's diet was slowly gathering momentum. After many meetings at the I.C.L., the milk pasteurization plant in Botoshani, the director gradually came round to agreeing that providing the children with fresh milk, cream, yoghurt and cheese would be a worthwhile humanitarian gesture. A refrigerated lorry drove every morning from Botoshani to supply the state shops in Dorohoi, a town to the north of Yonashen. If we paid for the extra fuel, the director suggested that this lorry could make a detour past the orphanage. Since the I.C.L. was a state company it would be fine to pay by cheque at the end of each month, and we worked out a system of daily deliveries that would supply the children with ample supplies of fresh dairy produce for less than 20 pounds a week.

I returned victorious to tell Mitica the good news, but met with nothing but predictions of disaster.

'What time will this milk be delivered?'

'Between six and seven in the morning.'

'But the kitchen staff don't start work till seven!'

My suggestion that another member of staff could unlock the kitchen door for the milkman was considered entirely impractical.

'This cream costs eighty *lei* a litre! The children don't need cream! The last thing you were telling me was that they have too much fat and cholesterol, yet now you tell me they need cream!'

I tried to explain that since a great deal of Romanian

cooking contains sour cream, it would be nice if the cooks had the opportunity to create the kind of meals for the children that they themselves would eat at home. When I had mentioned cream to Ili he had become quite carried away, reeling off the dishes he would be able to make if he had cream to work with.

I needed Mitica's signature on the contract I'd drawn up with the I.C.L. before the latter would commence deliveries, but he kept procrastinating, day after day claiming to be too busy and rushing in the opposite direction whenever he saw me. In the end it was the intervention of a Swedish nutritionist that persuaded him to sign; she was at Yonashen with the Star of Hope charity, a wealthy organization which had sent two nurses to work in *Copii Mici*, with the small children in the tower. The Star of Hope was holding out a huge carrot for Mitica regarding future plans. They were promising to finance the building of a new orphanage on the outskirts of Botoshani, to which most of the Yonashen children would be moved. Mitica would be the director, with all the status and prestige of being in control of what promised to be, if the plans were anything to go by, one of the most modern and deluxe establishments in Romania. Thus any suggestions or requests made by someone from the Star of Hope carried a great deal more weight than the same idea coming from one of us, a mere Brit with little to offer except enthusiasm. Still, on this occasion it forced Mitica to sign and I was grateful for the help (except when I later heard the said nutritionist tell a conference that she had started milk deliveries at Yonashen, when I became self-righteously furious – I began to understand why inter-charity relations are so notoriously petty).

So the dairy produce began arriving; the deliveries were never straightforward and, as Mitica had predicted, there were endless problems. If the driver was late setting off from Botoshani he wouldn't bother to make the detour, instead delivering twice as much the next day which couldn't all be fitted into the fridge; the milk was sometimes sour on arrival and Lenutsa would refuse to pay for it; they would forget to send the cream and Ili would be in a foul mood all day because he couldn't make the recipe that he'd been planning. But I was sure that in time it would all sort itself out and I felt confident enough to move on to the next item on my list: fruit and vegetables.

It was now mid-June and the produce appearing in Botoshani market was a chef's dream: tomatoes, cucumbers, aubergines, sweet peppers, zucchini, lettuces, radishes . . . There were cherries and plums, peaches and even some strawberries if you looked hard enough. The problem, however, lay in the fact that almost all of it came from private producers who would only accept cash. There were a few state shops selling fruit and vegetables but they tended to be more expensive and of infinitely inferior quality.

I knew that the state hotels and restaurants had access to good supplies, whilst their buyers must be under the same restrictions as Lenutsa. I asked the chef of the best restaurant in town where he bought his vegetables and was given the address of the I.C.L.F., the state-run fruit and vegetable depot. With Blondu and Florin in tow I managed to make an appointment with the director, who enthusiastically took us round store rooms filled with vast quantities of almost every fruit and vegetable that I'd seen in the market, at reasonable prices. He told me that weekly deliveries would be possible if we were prepared to pay for the fuel and I nearly hugged him.

We returned to his office to work out the details. The greatest problem lay in the fact that both stocks and prices changed daily so our orders would have to depend on what was available. The director suggested we set the amount that we were prepared to spend and they would send a different selection each week; I thought a better idea would be for us to ring each week to ascertain the current prices and place an order accordingly.

I drove back to Yonashen in high spirits and excitedly told my news to Lenutsa and Mitica. As usual they were unimpressed. Regarding the I.C.L.F. director's suggestion, they both said we would undoubtedly be dumped with all the rotten vegetables that no one else would buy, and my idea of ringing to find out the prices and then placing an order was considered far too complicated to be practicable. I was furious, which soon turned to depression as I went back to the drawing board and waited for another idea.

I worked out that at current Romanian prices, even if we bought expensive vegetables like tomatoes the total weekly bill wouldn't come to more than 10,000 *lei* – about 25 pounds. Over half could be bought at the state shops in town, and considering the amount of foreign food we were supplying anyway, I thought it would be worthwhile if we bought the remaining ten pounds' worth ourselves out of charity funds from private stallholders. I put the suggestion to Moona who agreed, and I returned to Mitica with an alternative proposal: I would drive Lenutsa into Botoshani each week, where she could buy what she could from the state shops with her cheques and I would buy what wasn't available to her in the market with our cash. He reluctantly agreed that it might work and I organized to drive into town with Lenutsa the next day.

By now I had grown to know Lenutsa relatively well. Like most of the staff at Yonashen, her principal concerns were her own home and family. The orphanage was merely her place of work, the source of her income, and she thought the emotional involvement of the volunteers was quite mad. Lenutsa was in her early forties and lived in Buchecha, the large village about five miles from Yonashen, with her four children and a husband who seemed to be continually ill and out of work. Thus she was both the principal breadwinner and a busy mother, and perhaps not surprisingly she wanted her job to be as hassle-free as possible. My attempts to shake up the entire way the children were fed continually exasperated her, but in a strange way we grew fond of each other over the summer. I was invited to her home and met her husband and her children. Her youngest ones were twin boys just starting school, and one of them was left-handed. His teachers were tying his left arm behind his back to force him to stop writing 'in the manner of the devil', and Lenutsa was entirely bewildered by my horror at such a mediaeval attitude.

On the day of our first shopping trip into Botoshani, it was unfortunately stiflingly hot and we didn't manage to leave Yonashen until almost midday. The sweat poured down Lenutsa's face and she did not share any of my glee as we scanned the town for the best deals and loaded the Land Rover with crates of beautiful vegetables. She was used to writing a single cheque to the storekeeper in Buchecha (with whatever scams I dreaded to imagine went on between them) and the idea of drafting endless small cheques to people she'd never met before seemed highly degrading to her. She also found it embarrassing being seen in a filthy old Land Rover surrounded by lettuces. When a slug crawled on to her she threatened to jump out and catch the bus home instead.

I was worried that the children, having perhaps never eaten fresh vegetables in their lives, would find them revolting and refuse to touch them – and I dreaded to think of the effect on their digestive systems, imagining that the new toilets would be put to a severe test. I was wrong, however. Ili, firmly on my side now that he could see that my endeavours were having some effect, produced absolutely delicious salads, complete with dressings and herbs, and the children stuffed them down with their customary lack of finesse, almost as if their little bodies knew how much they needed them.

◀ Peasant farmer with ox-cart in Transylvania

William making friends ▶

▲ Hannibal and author (*Times Newspapers*)

▲ Jacob - he and his family looked after me after the attack

▲ Yonashen Orphanage, Moldavia

Maureen in *Triaj* ▶

◀ Blondu sat on the Land Rover
with Susan in the background

▲ Florin (left) and Nicolae (*Andrew Crawley*)

▲ Evening entertainment - Colette and her guitar (*Wandsworth Charity Trust*)

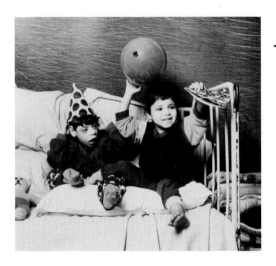

◄ Aurel (left) and Gabriella posing for photographs which appeared in an article about Yonashen in the *Mail On Sunday* magazine (*John Evans*)

Fiona ►

▲ Podriga, 'Psychiatric Section of Saveni Hospital'
(*Times Newspapers*)

▲ The Pavilion Children

Rob, the electrician, ▶
who ended up staying
six months

◀ Christy
(*Times Newspapers*)

▲ Down in the basement at Podriga, staying as close as
possible to the sorba for warmth
(*Times Newspapers*)

▲ In the upper rooms of Podriga, which were often kept locked
(*Times Newspapers*)

The day the children ate strawberries and cream for pudding I became quite emotional. They didn't like them nearly so much as the Mars Bars that were occasionally sent out on aid trucks, but this was a Romanian luxury they were eating that had been paid for by the Romanian Government, not a one-off humanitarian gesture from the West. In theory they could eat like this every week.

Therein lay the problem, however. In practice Lenutsa did everything possible to avoid letting me take her into Botoshani. She always claimed to be busy and it was never possible to set a time for going into town each week. She knew that she had me twisted round her little finger; I was so desperate to buy the food that she could set the times at her perfect convenience – usually when she had business of her own in Botoshani, or when she wanted a lift home and could be dropped off on her doorstep on the way back. It drove me mad and I often wished that I could go alone and simply pay for everything in cash; but since the whole object was to gradually remove the Romanians' reliance on us, I had to grit my teeth and continue my farcical, almost daily, Lenutsa chases.

It was the end of June and my time at Yonashen was nearly up. The thought of leaving made me feel depressed and miserable; I couldn't bear the idea of saying goodbye to Blondu, and my travels no longer held the promise of self-fulfilment that they once did. Although I was aware that I was probably being naive, I had a feeling that what I was doing here was the most worthwhile work I had ever done in my life. And, apart from that, I was quite simply enjoying myself. I loved kicking at a system that was so thoroughly rotten; I got a thrill out of the battle that made up for all the moments of frustration and self-doubt. And the chaos of Yonashen, that had so terrified me at the start, I had grown to love; I had never known a building so full of life and all the extremes of human nature.

One afternoon during what should have been my last week, I was sitting out in the garden in the hot summer sun talking to Moona. As we spoke about all that still needed to be done at Yonashen, he asked me if I would like to stay on longer. I didn't need much persuading; I promptly decided that I could postpone my travelling until the autumn and I said 'yes'. It would give me another six weeks to finish the work I'd started and by now I'd become involved with another matter that was growing increasingly difficult to solve, concerning a beautiful little four-year-old girl named Gabriella.

Chapter 6

Gabriella

In November 1990 Gabriella Constantin arrived at Yonashen from Dorohoi Hospital. Photographs taken of her at the time reveal a child resembling an Ethiopian famine victim, with bloated stomach, stick-like legs bowed by rickets, and terrified dark eyes staring up at the camera. She was four years old and she weighed just ten kilograms. The papers sent with her revealed only that she had been judged 'oligraphrenic' – a dated medical term meaning 'small-brained' – and that she had been a resident patient at Dorohoi Hospital since she was three months old.

Her grasp on life was so small that few at Yonashen dared to hope that she would live. Volunteers tried to take her to Botoshani Hospital for medical treatment but the doctors there refused to admit her, on the grounds that she was an 'irrecuperable' without a chance of survival. She returned to *Copii Mici* up in Yonashen's tower, where she refused to eat and screamed if anyone tried to touch her.

Susan Cooper, the young Scottish nurse who had told me the stories of Doamna Jetta on my first day, was working in *Copii Mici* at that time. Susan refused to give up on Gabriella, managing to forcefeed her with tiny amounts of milk by the hour. Over the next two weeks she hardly left the child's side, and she probably saved Gabriella's life. Slowly Gabriella began to trust her, letting Susan wash and change her, and in the third week she began to eat without being forced. Perhaps inevitably, a strong bond developed between Susan and Gabriella. Susan taught her how to walk, how to play, how to sing, and Gabriella adored her like a mother. When Susan returned home to Scotland for a break in the spring, she spoke incessantly of Gabriella to her parents.

Mr and Mrs Cooper have four children of their own and are experienced foster parents of problem and mentally retarded children. They decided to try to adopt Gabriella. If Susan had managed to keep this child alive, then they would like to give her the chance of a normal family life, away from the institutions of a country that did not seem to want her. They contacted their social services to seek approval as adoptive parents, and Susan returned to Yonashen hoping to sort out the Romanian side of officialdom.

When I met Susan she had come up against endless brick walls of bureaucracy. Her letters and phone calls of enquiry had all remained unanswered and she felt increasingly frustrated. Mitica had done nothing to help, and Susan's lack of transport had made it almost impossible for her to follow alternative avenues of investigation.

At home, my father had become involved in Romanian adoptions after a couple in his Parliamentary constituency had approached him for help soon after the 1989 revolution. Since then he had founded a pressure group, the Campaign for Inter-Country Adoption, to try to change the attitude of the British Government and social services towards those trying to adopt children from abroad. So now I rang him from a sweltering phone booth in Botoshani and asked him for his help.

The news was not good. From 1 June 1991 the Romanian Government had stopped all adoptions by foreigners while a new adoption law was being enacted. This was owing to the scandals arising from the black market 'baby trade' that had grown up since desperate and childless Western couples had arrived in Bucharest intending to save one of the orphans they had seen on their television screens back home. Orphanage directors had soon realized that these people had dollars in their pockets and invented endless hitches that could only be resolved by ever-increasing back-handers. The black marketeers soon got in on the act, 'buying' babies even before they were born, from desperate pregnant Romanian teenagers overwhelmed by the amounts of money being offered. The international press had discovered what was going on, and after a series of articles in influential papers, the Romanian Government closed its doors in a fit of embarrassment and hurt national pride.

The proposed new law seemed sensible: it confined adoptable children to those on a list drawn up from the orphanages, and all adoptions would have to be approved by the already established 'Adoption Committee' of child experts and lawyers in Bucharest. Astonishingly, however, the Romanian Parliament had rejected the law. Many politicians were known to be involved in the black market, and sinister forces were suspected to be at work to keep the former chaos alive, while at the other extreme fervent nationalists were trying to achieve a permanent ban on foreign adoptions, arguing that the country's youth was being stolen.

Thus the situation at present was in limbo. The Adoption Committee was trying to devise a law that might be acceptable to all factions in Parliament, and no one had a clue about when, if ever, foreign adoptions could begin again. The earliest date being given was October, but apparently even this was doubtful.

My father held out a hope for us, however. Apparently the Adoption Committee was still working on applications submitted before June, and it would listen to cases of urgency and extreme hardship. Dad gave me various names of people on the Committee and promised to find out as much as he could for us at home.

Susan was frantic. She was meant to be starting at university in October and understandably didn't want to leave Yonashen without Gabriella. With other children to look after at home, her mother could hardly come out to Romania for the months that it took to adopt a child through official channels; the work needed to be done by Susan while she was still in the country. And quite apart from that, if Gabriella was to be given the chance of a normal life, she needed to get on with it as soon as possible. She had already missed out on four years of the emotional and physical care that most of us take for granted; the Coopers were under no illusions that such deprivation would take a great deal of time to heal, and they wanted to turn the tide as soon as possible. Yonashen might have become a different place from the hell of pre-revolution days, but it was still a terrible place for a child to grow up in – sitting in a cot all day waiting for her half hour ration of individual attention from a face that changed from week to week.

Thus Susan and I grew determined that Gabriella should be accepted as a special case, and we made plans to go down to Bucharest to see the Adoption Committee and anyone else who might be able to help us.

Bucharest in summer was a different place from the grey miserable city of the previous December. After the primitive facilities in our northern corner of Moldavia, New York could not have seemed more full of wealth and opportunity. The parks were green and filled with students; we ate ice cream at the Athenae Palace Hotel, and there was a Stefanel shop just opened on the main boulevard where we marvelled that anyone could afford to pay the equivalent of 15 pounds for a shirt. Our eyes were agog at it all; we stared in awe at the smart diplomats' cars in front of the Bucharest Hotel and we took photos posing in front of one. We could buy whisky and vodka at the bars, even British cigarettes were now being sold.

I noticed a definite lowering of status, however, now that I was here as an aid worker rather than a journalist. Romanians knew that aid workers hardly had two *lei* to rub together, and we were treated accordingly. We weren't even let into the pretentious InterContinental Hotel – the doorman was entirely unmoved by the fact that we were working without pay to help his fellow countrymen, merely repeating that he would not let us in until we had changed into more expensive looking clothes.

Susan and I fought gallantly but unsuccessfully for entry into the Adoption Committee building. We tried again and again, posing over the phone as orphanage volunteers, would-be adopters, journalists, emissaries from the Secretariat for the Handicapped, and finally even British MPs, but all to no avail. The only information we gleaned from the voice on the phone was that the child must be one from 'the list'. We asked how we might find out whether Gabriella was on it, but were told that *we* don't choose our child – it is assigned to us by the committee, and all our dealings must be conducted through an approved international adoption agency from our country of origin. We tried to explain that there were special circumstances but the line was abruptly cut and we had no further success.

Other sources revealed that the proposed law we had been outlined, albeit rather abruptly, had just been rejected by Parliament. Apparently changes to the Bill were unlikely to alter most of these details; rather, it seemed, many more restrictions would be added to it.

I rang my father again, who had little hope to offer. He was currently trying to persuade the British Government to prepare itself for the new Romanian law, since Britain didn't even *have* an approved international adoption agency. Unfortunately, however, most of the Social Service departments seemed to think this was a brilliant excuse for stopping Romanian adoptions in Britain altogether (for the Social Services they had never meant anything but extra work), and the Health Ministry was currently doing absolutely nothing for the hundreds of couples who would be affected by the Adoption Committee's new demands.

We sought other avenues of information; unfortunately most of the journalists I had met in December were now in Yugoslavia covering the civil war, but we heard again and again that adoptions were still taking place under the old law if you knew the right channels.

The old law had demanded that a 'Home Study' be carried out by a Romanian lawyer, paid by the prospective adopters, to show that the child was 'adoptable'. This had to prove the existence of the original birth certificate and include a signed release from the natural parents, confirming that they were unable to support the child and were not interested in it. The would-be parents had to have approval from their Social Services at home as suitable adopters, presented in a corresponding Home Study report. Otherwise nothing was necessary save endless bribes – the orphanage director wouldn't find the names of the parents unless it was made worth his while; the mother often asked for money for the trouble of signing the release form; lawyers' fees were payable only in US dollars, over half of which were taken as 'tax' by the Government; and court officials often demanded money to speed up the proposed hearing from an originally proposed date of anything up to a year hence.

The irony of this system was that a child whose parents could not be traced was extremely hard to adopt. Many women who had abandoned their babies in orphanages had given false identities and could never be found; thus it was often easier to adopt a child by buying one straight from an impoverished family than by trying to rescue one from an orphanage, where many of the mothers named on the birth certificates had never even existed. For such a child to be 'adoptable' you had to prove legal abandonment through yet more costly and time consuming procedures.

But at least the old system meant that genuine cases who fought hard enough usually managed to adopt their baby in the end. Up until now, for most British adopters, the greatest hurdle had been getting through the Social Services at home who weren't much better than the Romanians in that they were demanding anything up to 4,000 pounds to carry out the necessary Home Study survey, and some regions were refusing to do them at all on political grounds.

We began seeing lawyers, who for amounts varying between 10,000 and 50,000 dollars said they could 'get our baby for us'. Without exception this meant faking and backdating papers; if it had been left to us, I think Susan and I would have tried to haggle the price down and give it a try, but the Coopers were adamant that everything should be done legally and properly, without bribes.

Susan was inevitably feeling depressed by all the closed doors, so Jon and I spent the weekend trying to cheer her up, going to a terrifying funfair in Bucharest's central park and wandering round the haunting 'Village Museum'. Ceauşescu, presumably so that there was still some record of them when he had succeeded in destroying all the old villages, had transported genuine examples of every type of peasant house from all the various regions of Romania to an area in the middle of Bucharest. It was haunting to find exact replicas of the houses we were living in up in Moldavia; what was our reality was in a museum, as if officially it no longer really existed.

Susan and I hired a boat on one of the park's lakes, soon finding ourselves surrounded by Romanian youths who pelted water at us with their oars and were seemingly intent on capsizing our boat. We were rescued by a Westerner who turned out to be a true knight in shining armour – he was an American lawyer, and back on shore, he listened to our tales of woe with surprising sympathy and optimism. He said that yes, adoptions were still going ahead under a strange combination of the old and new laws. Since ours seemed such a deserving case, he said he would give us what help he could. We gave him all the details, but the vital unknown was whether Gabriella was on the Adoption Committee's list – if not, he said we must get her on to it as soon as possible, with a special recommendation from the orphanage director explaining the special circumstances of the case and the fact that this particular child was wanted for adoption by a named couple with personal connections to it. He advised us that we must find Gabriella's birth certificate and – the most onerous task of all – seek out her parents to see whether they were willing for her to be adopted.

We sought the help of the Secretariat for the Handicapped, the body ultimately responsible for the children at Yonashen, who informed us that all children who would be regarded as 'adoptable' under the proposed new law – if they were true orphans or had been abandoned for at least two years – should now be on the list of available children at the Adoption Committee. Apparently there was nothing to stop handicapped children from being adoptable, and the director of Yonashen should have compiled a list and sent it to Bucharest some months ago. They had no idea though whether he had actually done so.

We returned to the Adoption Committee building, desperate to find out if Gabriella was on the list.

'Not unless her name has been submitted by the director of her institution,' we were told.

'How can we find out whether this was done?'

'Ask him,' came the (fairly logical) reply.

So we returned to Yonashen with something like a plan

of campaign. Mitica didn't even have the grace to be embarrassed as he told us that he had not compiled a list of adoptable children. He thought he might have received a letter about it a while ago, he said, but he had thrown it away without a moment's thought. At first I thought he was joking, as he told us that nothing we said could persuade him to help the Coopers adopt Gabriella, for he had a smile on his face and seemed to find our earnestness amusing. Slowly we realized that he was serious. As we tried to state our case more persuasively, he lost his grin and became more adamant.

His reasons varied from the opinion that there wasn't a single adoptable child at Yonashen, due to their all being handicapped – apparently no normal, unperverted couple could possibly want one of them – to his vehemently expressed belief, which to me sounded like twisted resentment of the West but to Mitica was nothing but the best kind of patriotism, that they were Romanian children and thus should stay in Romania.

'How dare Westerners think they can march in and take away the bloom of Romania's youth?'

The fact that this particular bloom would probably have died were it not for Susan seemed to have escaped him. No, he said, he would not compile a list. He was the children's legal guardian and he did not want them to be adopted by foreigners.

Susan was close to tears and we beat a retreat from Mitica's office. We were determined to win him round somehow, and Susan, with the help of one of the Romanian medical assistants, began compiling the list herself. She spent hours going through social and medical records stored away in dusty cupboards, periodically coming up for air in the volunteers' room looking very pale and shocked. They made depressing reading, due to the fact that the majority of entries, next to the list of the hundreds of children who had made the fateful step through the gates of Yonashen, were 'DECEDAT' – 'deceased'. We worked out that during the Ceauşescu years roughly a third of Yonashen's children had died each winter. The cause of death was rarely detailed. Occasionally it was noted that the child's family had come to take the body away, but usually they were just buried at the local churchyard in unmarked graves.

I found Florin's details and discovered that a sick twist of fate had given him the same surname as the President – Iliescu. He was born on 5 April 1978 and had arrived at Yonashen in 1982 from *Leagunul Numero Uno* – Baby Orphanage No 1 – in Botoshani. Medical details were confined to his simple categorization as 'oligraphrenic'. There was no information about his mother, but the medical assistant thought that there would probably be more at the baby orphanage.

For Gabriella there was more: her parents were named as Gheorghe and Maria Constantin, and there was the name of a village, Mihaeleni, about 15 miles from Yonashen. Mimica, the medical assistant, agreed to accompany us there the next day to try to find them, and Susan and I grew increasingly nervous about the prospect of actually meeting and speaking to Gabriella's parents.

We drove through Mihaeleni to the mayor's office and tried to leave most of the talking to Mimica, having instructed her not to mention anything about adoption. We'd been warned that, if we did find them, Gabriella's parents would almost certain demand money in return for their permission, so we wanted to successfully track them down before any word of possible adoptions got around the neighbourhood.

The mayor knew an old gypsy couple called Constantin and was sure they had a son called Gheorghe. He gave us the address and we set off to the opposite end of the village. We found a normal house with ducks and chickens in the yard outside. It was perhaps a little scruffier than most, with chipped paint and a collapsing fence, but no more so than many I had come across on my travels. Had I known nothing of the circumstances, I would have expected the house to contain an ordinary peasant family.

A nice-looking old man came out and eyed us with suspicion as Mimica asked whether he had a son called Gheorghe who had once had a daughter called Gabriella. Yes, he said. He then asked who wanted to know and Mimica explained that Gabriella was under her care at Yonashen. This was enough for the old man to send another of his sons with us in the Land Rover to try to find Gheorghe. He worked at the collective farm, the old man said – as a good third of the men in the village probably did. We finally tracked him down on the hill above the town, with a pretty woman with long black plaits down to her waist. Susan grew visibly nervous; neither of us had expected it to be so easy to find Gabriella's parents and we both felt at a loss regarding how to ask the necessary questions.

Gheorghe looked barely thirty. He was a handsome man – we instantly recognized Gabriella's physical appeal – with classic gypsy looks – a mass of jet black hair and beautiful brown eyes. He was small, probably not even as tall as me, with a wiry, athletic build. He smiled at us and jumped into the Land Rover, happily accompanying us back to the family home where he still lived with his parents. When we broached the subject of Gabriella he appeared totally unfazed; there was no sign at all of embarrassment or distress. He seemed interested to know how Gabriella was; and what about Georgina? How was she?

'Georgina?'

It turned out that there were two daughters who had both been handed into care, as well as a son who Gheorghe had been informed had died at one of the orphanages in Botoshani the previous year. He told us all this very matter of factly, with none of the shame and embarrassment that

I had expected. As we tried to broach the subject of *why* they had been put into care, we discovered that the woman we had seen with him on the hill was not the children's mother. 'She' had gone off, apparently, to somewhere in the middle of the country; 'she' had been a terrible mother and hadn't wanted the children. Gheorghe seemed to take it for granted that his wife was the one responsible for them, that if she didn't want them there was nothing he could do to help them; it seemed entirely natural to him and certainly nothing to be ashamed about.

This at least made it easier to broach the subject of adoption. He said immediately that it would be fine by him; ironically it was *his* parents who were much more wary. Gabriella's grandfather told us that he had heard that children were being shipped abroad to be used for 'spare parts' – this transpired to mean using organs for transplants, plus making soap from the bones. Her grandmother had heard that Romanian girls were being used as unpaid servants in Western households. We tried to reassure them, explaining that it was Susan's parents who wanted to adopt Gabriella, that they were good Christian people who wanted to bring her up as one of their own, to offer her a better life than she could ever have at Yonashen. We were both touched that they at least seemed so genuinely concerned about their grandchild's welfare. As they spoke of Gabriella I realized they had no idea of the kind of conditions that she had been living in. They seemed to imagine that she was being well-cared for and educated and, especially now that foreigners were at Yonashen, they thought her life must be much more luxurious than anything they could have provided.

Gheorghe was sure that Gabriella's mother would give her permission for the adoption.

'She hasn't a mother's heart,' he said. 'She never loved them.'

He had the phone number of the co-operative farm

where she worked but no address, so he came with us to the telephone exchange in the centre of the village to try to establish some contact. He spoke to the manager and scribbled down the address of a farm near Bacchau, about 200 miles south of Botoshani, handing it to Susan and wishing her luck.

We both found it impossible to dislike Gheorghe, despite the fact that he had so unashamedly put his three children into care, or 'lack of care' as Susan put it. He was friendly and helpful, searching through the house to see if he had the children's birth certificates. He couldn't find them, however, and said that their mother must have them. Georgina was about three, he thought, and he managed to find a letter saying that she was at *Leagunul Numero Doi* – Baby Orphanage No 2 – in Botoshani. He asked Susan if her parents would like to adopt both the girls; Georgina was a much better bet, he thought, for she'd been a much healthier baby than Gabriella.

We returned to Yonashen hardly able to contain our curiosity, and within an hour we'd found an excuse to drive into Botoshani. Neither of us knew where the baby orphanages were but enquiries at the hospital led us to find Orphanage No 2 down a back street in the centre of town. It was a modern building stuck amongst the towerblocks. We parked the Land Rover and knocked at the front door with a feeling of dread. As we were let in by a smartly uniformed nurse, however, we looked around in relief – it was a cheerful, brightly painted place. There was evidence of foreign aid – French posters covered the walls and small children were playing with Western toys. Over a hundred children, aged up to three years old, were crowded in with the cots jammed up against each other, but compared to Yonashen it was clean and very well-equipped, and there appeared to be a large number of staff at work.

We asked after Gabriella's sister.

'Yes,' one of the staff told us, 'we have a Georgina

Constantin here – I'll go and fetch her.' There was no enquiry as to who we were or why we wanted to see her, and within five minutes a bigger, fatter version of Gabriella was handed to us. The likeness was astonishing; she had just the same big brown wary eyes and stubborn little mouth. As she played with her, Susan grew rather weepy.

'Oh God, Sophie, we can't take one home and leave the other behind here. She'll probably be sent to Yonashen next year, and I couldn't live with myself knowing we'd left Gabriella's sister behind.'

Since we didn't seem to be having much luck getting even one of them out, I kept quiet, not wanting to say anything that might fire Susan's hopes. One of the nurses then asked us why we were interested in Georgina – did we want to adopt her?

'Maybe,' said Susan, before I could stop her.

'But why?' replied the nurse, appearing genuinely astonished. 'She's a gypsy child, and she'll grow up to be a gypsy. We've got plenty of Romanian children here – surely you'd rather have one of them?'

She returned a few minutes later with a blond-haired, blue-eyed little boy of about the same age. 'Isn't he lovely? Wouldn't you rather have this one?'

We were both rendered speechless, and simply began playing with both of them. Neither of us were prepared for the bombshell that came next, however. Susan asked about the nature of foreign aid work at the orphanage and was told that it was being run by a French organization and was mainly to do with 'SIDA' – AIDS.

'Oh,' Susan said, trying to remain calm. 'Is that a big problem here?'

We were then told that almost half of the two hundred children were thought to be HIV positive – and yes, some of them had full-blown AIDS.

'What about Georgina?'

The nurse wasn't sure and went off to find out; we heard a heated argument concerning the whereabouts of a list, and then she returned with a medical assistant wielding some typed sheets of paper. They sat down and searched through it, finally looking up triumphantly.

'Here we are, Constantin, Georgina. Yes, she is HIV positive.'

Our journey home was made in silence. We were both shocked and could feel little except terrible sadness, that a small child who had little enough going for her anyway should have been infected with a disease that in the next few years would probably kill her.

It wasn't till another visit to Bucharest a few weeks later that I found out from an English journalist investigating the matter why the AIDS figures in an orphanage should be so high. The staff at Orphanage No 2 had told us that it was because the mothers of these children were 'bad women' – gypsies and whores and drug abusers – but this hardly seemed plausible. I found it difficult to believe that a hard drug had ever been seen in Botoshani – they didn't even smoke the marijuana growing in their fields. However, I knew that sterilization of instruments was a rare thing to be found in hospitals, and I suspected that this was more likely to be the source.

In Bucharest I discovered that there still exists in Romania the medical belief that an underweight baby can be helped by an immediate injection of blood. Apparently this practice was given up in Britain before the war as being more likely to cause harm than good, but in Romania it goes on. At the same time, blood for transfusion is still not tested for AIDS or hepatitis. Thus every day hundreds of premature or underweight newborn babies are stuffed with possibly HIV-infected blood, and no one is doing anything to stop it. The journalist I spoke to was convinced this was because the Romanian Government saw it as an easy solution to their orphanage problem; since the children abandoned in orphanages come from the least privileged section of Romanian society, they are much more likely than most to be underweight at birth. I found this too disturbing a thought even to contemplate, but I did feel incredibly angry at such an unnecessary waste of lives, whether or not there was a hidden motive behind it.

The Yonashen children had been AIDS tested and, miraculously it now seemed, were all free from infection. Ironically, the refusal of hospitals to treat 'irrecuperables' had proved to be their saving; once inside the walls of Yonashen the children had lived and died there, without any contact with the outside world. It had meant that many had probably died of easily treatable diseases, but at least they hadn't been exposed to the HIV virus.

I was away in Bucharest when Susan went down to Bacchau to visit the mother of Gabriella and Georgina. She took with her Dino, a young journalist from Botoshani who had worked at Yonashen as a translator in the early days of the volunteer presence. They had found a very attractive woman living with a man to whom both of them took an instant dislike. Maria had at first seemed willing to consent to the adoption of both children, but then the man had become involved, demanding large sums of money. Unfortunately Dino then lost his temper and became abusive, telling them exactly what he thought of them – criticizing them as people who would give up their children, then demand money in return for their going to a good home. He also referred to them as gypsies, the inevitable racism showing through in his anger. Susan returned to Yonashen furious with Dino for possibly ruining our chances altogether, and upset that we hadn't even been able to get past this first hurdle of parental consent.

Susan's parents came out to Yonashen in August. They instantly fell in love with Gabriella, who by now was walking, had overcome her great fear of the outdoors enough to play in the garden and was speaking more and more each day. Mr and Mrs Cooper spoke to lawyers and officials at the *Prefectura* and, considering the fact that Gabriella's mother was unwilling to give her consent, and their Social Services at home were refusing to complete a Home Study report until the new Romanian law was enacted and functioning, they decided they had little choice but to wait. Even so, their charm did persuade Mitica to submit to Bucharest a complete list of Yonashen's adoptable children.

In November 1992 the Romanian Parliament finally gave approval to the Bucharest Adoption Committee's revised proposals for a new adoption law. One of the law's new sections stipulated that no foreign couple aged over thirty-five and forty respectively for the mother and father could under any circumstances adopt a Romanian child. Margaret and Bill Cooper are both over forty.

Chapter 7

Deepening Bonds

Over the summer the other volunteers at Yonashen became
good friends. We were an extraordinary bunch, I suppose
– a strange mixture of professionals and enthusiastic amateurs from diverse walks of life. At Yonashen backgrounds
and ages ceased to matter, and friendships were made that
would perhaps never stand a chance at home. Almost all
the volunteers were very different from the goody-goody
types I had expected; in fact there was a definite lack of
self-righteous earnestness. Most wanted to have fun whilst
they were in Romania, and both work and play were
usually injected with an extraordinary amount of singing
and laughter.

Most of the volunteers lived with Romanian families in
the village of Yonashen, but a few rented houses of their
own and in the evenings we would congregate at one or
other of these. Watching the beautiful summer sunsets
across the valley, we'd relax over a few beers away from
the chaos of our days at the orphanage. Sometimes we'd
throw a barbecue and villagers would come along too
with the obligatory bottle of *tsuica*. The weekends were
dominated by the endless stream of weddings to which
we were always invited. Almost half the orphanage staff
and most of the young people in the village seemed to
be getting married that summer, in ceremonies and great
feastings that lasted a minimum of twenty-four hours at

which we had to at least make an appearance so as not to insult the newlyweds and their families.

One evening, a few weeks after my arrival, I was having a beer in the garden of Issy's house in the village and I began talking to a girl whom I'd noticed in the volunteers' room but hadn't yet spoken to. She was a pretty, Eastern-looking girl called Evie, and she was one of the few volunteers with an English accent. On this particular evening she was looking pale and in shock, just having returned from Botoshani Hospital with one of the Front Section children, Christina, who had a broken thumb.

They had been directed to the operating room where the doctor signalled to Evie to wait in the corner while he finished operating on a boy's foot. The boy obviously had had no anaesthetic for he was screaming loudly, clutching on to his mother who looked equally terrified as the doctor dug around with his scalpel. The whole room was filthy; blood dripped on to the floor and both staff and patients frequently wandered in and out. When he'd finished on the boy, the doctor told the mother to take her son back to the ward for stitches, and he hobbled out, leaving a trail of blood to the door. The doctor put down his instruments, lit a cigarette and came over to talk to Evie, agreeing to set Christina's thumb once he had finished with his next patient, a baby girl, whose throat he began prodding while the cigarette was still in his hand. He stamped out the cigarette on the floor before picking up his instruments, still bloody from the boy's foot, and jammed them into the baby's mouth.

Christina by this stage was almost hysterical and began screaming when she realized that she was the next in line. In the process she managed to hurl herself from the bench where Evie had sat her, banging her head against a table in front of her which started a violent nosebleed, accompanied by increasingly violent yells. Seeing the baby practically choking under the doctor's nicotine-stained hands, Evie picked up Christina and ran out of the building, and returned to Yonashen with a child far less well than when she had left. Fiona managed to bind up her thumb with splints and bandages, and Evie escaped to the village in search of a much-needed drink.

Evie was typical of many of the volunteers in that she had originally come to Yonashen for a short stint but had found it impossible to leave. By now her six weeks had turned into four months and, like many, she planned to stay for as long as her money supply held out. When I asked her what she did at home, she said, 'Don't ask, I was part of the most unpopular profession in London.'

My assumption that she must have been a traffic warden produced loud guffaws. In fact she'd been an estate agent, a long way from London property as we sat outside a wattle and daub peasant's dwelling in the middle of Moldavia. Although on paper unqualified, she was brilliant with the kids; she worked with the small children in *Copii Mici* and the older ones in Front Section, and was always amazingly full of energy. Over the summer she became a very good friend. She looked after the dogs for me when I had to go to Bucharest, becoming almost as potty about them as I was, and she proved to be a loyal shoulder to cry on whenever I became over-emotional about the children.

I translated regularly for some of the girls working in the Sections. I found it a humbling experience seeing how they coped with the children, forcing me to realize that I wasn't capable of what they were doing. They worked long shifts trying to give equal attention to far too many children, each of whom demanded full-time care that it just wasn't possible to give. I knew I didn't have the patience or the professionalism to have been able to do it; my own brief ventures into the Sections always left me feeling totally shattered and exhausted, both mentally and physically.

One of the ironies of the volunteer presence was that the children had grown much more unruly and badly behaved.

During the times when the Romanian staff were left in charge, all would be sitting quietly in their designated spot and there would be an air of peace and tranquillity. When volunteers were around though, the children knew they would not be hit or beaten and they expressed their desire for attention and curiosity for new experiences as boisterously as they could. Not surprisingly it was extremely difficult to convince the Romanian staff that our methods were best, and at times it was hard not to be doubtful ourselves. To reverse the harm caused by a lifetime's emotional and physical deprivation would take years; we all knew this, yet sometimes it was impossible not to be depressed by the lack of changes. Periodically each one of us would be overwhelmed by the feeling that the task was too great and our individual contributions worthless. At times I was convinced that every change I was trying to bring about was sure to be abandoned as soon as I had left – so what was the point of trying?

Whenever I felt myself growing depressed I would find myself almost miraculously surrounded by friends, even though I hadn't said a word to anyone about how I felt. Amongst the volunteers there was an unspoken support system to help each other over the periods of doubt and despair: because each one of us went through them, it was as if we could automatically sense when it was happening to someone else and would band together to convince them that the effort they were making was worthwhile. It was an extraordinary bond, and even those who didn't get on would reach out to help each other when one of them was down. This support became especially strong – and necessary – when we later moved to Podriga, an adult institution about sixty miles from us, but I noticed it from the start, this emotional closeness we all shared from being stuck in a remote part of a strange country whose inhabitants regarded us as either mad or absurdly naïve.

A person to lift everyone's spirits was Colette Hughes,

the girl who spent most of her evenings chasing Blondu down from the roof. I was terrified of her at first; she looked tough as nails, with a strong Belfast accent and paint-spattered jeans, but I came to see her as rather like William, a poodle in Dobermann's clothing who would always help you out in times of trouble. She played the guitar and had the voice of an angel. On a Sunday when the rest of us were enjoying a long lie in bed she could always be found up at the orphanage singing to the children, holding even the most difficult children in spellbound silence. The best evenings were always those down at Emma's house in Virfu Cimpului, when she sat on the bed by the stove and did her best to play our requested tunes, not stopping till her voice was hoarse. A group of her friends came out from Belfast for a fortnight in July to work at Yonashen doing any grotty jobs they could find, and they gave us the best two weeks of the summer. The orphanage was constantly filled with music and singing; the enthusiasm of the Irish encouraged everyone to work till past nine in the evening.

Though we weren't so aware of it at the time, the changes at Yonashen came thick and fast over the summer. There were never enough funds and our work was always frustratingly piecemeal; we heard of large projects going on at orphanages which had the backing of the large charities – the Romanian Orphanage Trust and the *Daily Mail*'s Romanian Angel Appeal – with unmitigated envy, begging for their left-over supplies like poor relations. Our own funding came from four small groups in Dublin, Belfast, Edinburgh and London – ordinary people who worked voluntarily in their free time to provide our endless stream of requests for building materials, electrical equipment, medical supplies, nappies, food, money . . . and slowly it was all producing results. The plumbing installed in June changed the reality of life at Yonashen almost beyond belief. At last the endemic lice and scabies could be kept under control; showering became a pleasurable event for the children to look forward to and enjoy, and they suddenly both looked and smelt much more lovable. You no longer had to hold your nose as you walked down the Front Corridor past the loos; the staff were so amazed by what was for some of them the first upright toilets and hot showers they had ever seen, that they kept them spotless. The new plumbing proved to be the trigger for a huge improvement in general hygiene. Now that their bodies smelt of roses there seemed more point in trying to keep the children in clean clothes; bottoms could be washed between nappy changes, while sores and cuts suddenly began healing much more quickly.

The transition to Western methods of hygiene proved to be a complicated process for some of the children, however, especially for the more seriously disturbed children in *Triaj*. A relatively stable little boy called Ion was put on to the loo every day after lunch for his daily bowel movement, but as soon as the volunteer had moved her attention to someone else, he would leap off and make a very neat little pile of pooh on the floor next to the toilet. It proved very difficult explaining to him that he hadn't quite got it right yet, since he'd at least been in the correct room and very close to the appointed place, which was much better than what most of his still nappy-bound room-mates could manage.

Loo roll, likewise, proved to be a disaster. From the children's point of view it was one of the best games ever invented, but it caused the first major blockage of the new pipe system and wedges of it could be found for weeks afterwards spouting from choking plugholes.

A new pump down at the well in the valley improved the water supply immeasurably, except when it rained heavily, which never failed to cause an immediate drought inside the building. I confess to this having flummoxed me completely until I learnt that the pump's failure was due not to any lack of water but to a short circuiting of the electricity supply due to the excess rain.

Moona persuaded the Botoshani Electricity Board to fork out for miles of new wiring plus all the necessary pylons and transformers so that Yonashen could be supplied with three-phase power. The first and greatest result of this was that we could now make use of the new laundry – industrial washing machines and dryers that had been shipped out from Ireland in a container. Up until now we had only been able to look at them in frustrated agony as the old boiler in the basement continued to ruin all the donated clothes. The appearance of the children changed overnight as suddenly the whites stayed white instead of turning a universal muddy grey after the first wash; buttons stayed on and zips kept working, jumpers didn't all end up in the small children's section (*Copii Mici*) after being shrunk, and in wet weather there were no longer vast amounts of dripping laundry hung around the building drying. The constant nappy shortage was resolved too, for now we could use Terrys instead of having to rely on disposables from the West.

In August a religious group came out from Britain to build a 'rehab centre' for the older children in just two weeks. Children and volunteers alike watched in amazement as at astonishing speed a bungalow grew up in the grounds at the back of the orphanage. Danny, one of the plumbers from June, came out to fit it with a kitchen and bathroom. Over the next month we kitted it out with stoves, furniture, curtains, and even a garden fence – the children thought we'd finally gone mad. Finally it was ready. Under the direction of Diane, a physiotherapist who had come out in July with boundless resources of energy and ideas, it was put to use as an activity centre in an attempt to teach the children the social skills they would need if they were ever to survive in the outside world. Extraordinary culinary concoctions began arriving as 'presents' in the volunteers' room, along with paintings and pieces of woodwork.

As more young children arrived at Yonashen, the question of the older ones 'moving on' was forced upon us by Mitica and the system that we spent most of our time pretending we were not a part of. In a country without any social services or welfare there was not a hope that at eighteen the children from Yonashen could suddenly go out into the world. The new activity centre would, we hoped, enable them to fend for themselves and make a link with the outside. But at present they were all meant to go on to one of the adult 'psychiatric' institutions in the area, which would be their home for the rest of their lives. I'd heard of a few of them – two called Adashen and Podriga up in the north near the Soviet border, and one called Costina where a very brave English girl called Victoria Hornby was trying to introduce an aid project. They all sounded horrific and we fought to keep the children at Yonashen, offering to build a new wing, do anything that would make our four walls a safe haven for ever, for the kids we had grown to love. We managed reprieve after reprieve but finally at the end of August ten seriously disturbed children in *Triaj* were sent to Adashen. I was away when it happened and saw only Emma's tears afterwards. Like everyone else I tried to bury the thought of the children's future in the back of my mind, convincing myself that these places couldn't really be that bad, that we weren't really throwing them back into hell.

Other changes at Yonashen were purely down to the volunteers' own efforts – Linda managed to wean almost all of the younger children from their total dependence on powdered milk, Gabriella being a stubborn exception. Jackie and her team in *Triaj* struggled on without any of the glory – any success story they had was instantly taken from them, as a child who made great improvements was moved into the Front Section where the more capable children were. With everlasting patience they tried to persuade the staff that the *Triaj* children were worth spending time with, no matter how handicapped or disturbed they may have been.

One of the projects I enjoyed helping with was started by a highly experienced nurse called Annie, who had worked in Ethiopia with the Band Aid teams and always had an abundance of ideas on how to achieve changes without the backing of Western health care facilities. In her late twenties, Annie was a very pretty girl with long dark hair, and was an inspiration to many of us with less experience. Whereas Fiona worked largely alone, Annie worked directly with the volunteers and Romanian staff in the sections, giving medical advice and practical suggestions. She was lively and funny, and with her mixture of enthusiasm and professionalism she managed to achieve a level of co-operation from the Romanian staff that was envied by the rest of us. She began many successful programmes, one of which was her fight to win special treatment for the adolescent girls of the Front Section. Up till now they had been allowed no sense of any female identity, their monthly periods being a messy source of embarrassment and their breasts regarded as unwelcome parts of the body hard to fit into the small children's clothes delivered by the aid trucks. Annie began introducing ideas of personal hygiene and fought for permission to let them grow their hair. She searched through the aid parcels for skirts, dresses and pretty blouses, and introduced the wearing of pants and bras. Sanitary towels proved to be a problem; they are such a valuable commodity in Romania that they rarely got past the staff and, if they did, the younger children found them to be wonderful toys to be stuck on ceilings and on staff members' bottoms.

My own work gradually broadened from my original food finding missions. As well as harassing the Adoption Committee in Bucharest, I accompanied Moona and Fiona to the offices of the Secretariat for the Handicapped, the part of the Ministry of Works that was responsible for the running of institutions like Yonashen. Fiona was trying to promote the introduction of a national training programme for orphanage care workers, on the grounds that we would never be able to leave until a suitable Romanian-run system was established. The only trained staff currently at Yonashen were the two medical assistants, who sat upstairs drinking coffee all day because they considered themselves above physical involvement with the children. Fiona was trying to introduce teaching programmes for the staff, based on a differentiation between cleaners and carers, something that was not recognized by the current Romanian structure, and a defined career structure. At present the younger care workers, who usually had much better attitudes towards the children, spent their time endlessly cleaning the floors, while the older women saw themselves as responsible for disciplining the children and often did very little else.

Fiona had made detailed proposals for pilot training schemes which she gave to the relevant ministers in Bucharest. Their reaction was typically frustrating; they listened to her gravely, nodding their heads in agreement to every word, before taking the reports, painstakingly translated and copied on an old manual typewriter by those of us amongst the volunteers who could type, and filing them away in a drawer to lie unopened until our next visit.

I spoke to others at the Secretariat in Bucharest in an attempt to establish a legal status for our volunteer presence at Yonashen. Almost weekly Mitica made serious threats to throw us all out, whenever we did something he didn't approve of or questioned his judgement too closely, and we needed sanctioning from a higher authority to secure access to our own supplies and ensure we could finish the projects we had started. I also sought authorized access to the orphanage accounts. After discovering the discrepancy in the food allowance I was deeply suspicious of the whole set-up. Neither Doamna Jetta nor Mitica would let me go through the files in the accounts room, nor would they even explain the entitlements for the various areas of orphanage management – heating, repairs, clothing and so on. I felt that we couldn't budget our donations properly without knowing what the children were entitled to from the state, yet it seemed impossible to find out. Mitica was forever asking for money for all manner of things – light bulbs, bedding, office paper, telephone bills – which I found hard to believe were not provided for by the Government. But Mitica was always very understanding of his Government's problems; whenever we begged him to apply to Bucharest for a contribution to a project, he would quote to us the latest trade deficit and national debt figures, explaining as if to children that the Secretariat simply didn't have enough money. I thought with longing of the constant demands and criticism of the Government made by hospital chiefs back home as I tried to explain to Mitica that it wasn't his job to save Romania from its economic nightmare – it was his job to fight for what he could on behalf of the children.

The Bucharest ministers were just as adamant as the Yonashen management that we did not need to know Yonashen's legal entitlements. I slowly realized that the Secretariat for the Handicapped did not have a budget at all for its orphanages. The European Community was paying all the heating and fuel bills, and the message to the directors seemed to be little more than 'Get out of the foreigners all you can'. Apart from the 20 pence a day food quota (half of which was not being spent on the children if my experience was anything to go by), the Romanian Government was undertaking to do absolutely nothing for its estimated 140,000 orphans (they still didn't know how many they had).

Short of attempting a second revolutionary coup there was evidently nothing I could do legally to force them to contribute to our efforts at Yonashen. They had us twisted round their little fingers, since they realized we knew that if we pulled out they wouldn't step in with projects of their own. Fiona kept pestering them about the training programme and I hired a good lawyer in Botoshani to establish our presence at Yonashen in the form of a contract, but it continued to rankle that we were the paymasters, yet we had no authority. Mitica continued to insist that we seek his permission for everything we did short of going to the loo, and the accounts department remained a closed door to us.

Chapter 8

Hospital Nightmare

Soon after my arrival at Yonashen I moved to a small house up in the village. There was a garden where I could leave the dogs while I was working and a family nearby who looked after Hannibal for me, their son taking him down to the valley each day to graze and then riding him back each evening. My house had no water and no electricity; lighting was by candle, which was romantic for a while but the wax everywhere soon got on my nerves. I whitewashed the wattle and daub walls inside to improve the light, using Blondu and Florin's over-enthusiastic and unpaid child labour to get it done in a day. It was a day I've never forgotten, when a bond of understanding suddenly developed between Florin and me which shall forever make me feel guilty for not doing more to help him.

As usual a group of village children were hanging around the house, some of them helping us paint. Nicoletta, the sister of the boy who looked after Hannibal for me, began taunting Florin, with that unthinking cruelty unique to children.

'Why don't you talk? Go on, say something – you must be really stupid if you can't say anything at all. You're just like all the other morons at the orphanage, you haven't got a brain . . . you're really stupid, I bet you don't even understand what I'm saying, moron . . .'

Florin ignored it, turning the other cheek and pretending

that he didn't understand, but I flipped. I flew at her, telling her that she was an ignorant little bitch, that Florin was much more intelligent than any of them, that he'd lived through a hell that she couldn't even begin to imagine, that one day he *would* speak and he would put them all to shame. I ordered them all out of the house and told them they could come back when they'd learned how to be civil to my friends.

I half-expected Florin to be furious with me for embarrassing him. He'd walked out into the garden in the middle of my speech and I went out to join him, ready to apologize. He flew at me and I prepared myself for a punch, but instead I found that he had his arms tight around me and was clinging on to me in a bear hug. I hugged him back, pretending not to notice the tears landing on my shoulder, and we stayed like that for a while, clinging on to each other, until Florin finally pulled away and gave me a big smile.

I'd never known him give such a show of affection and I was moved almost to tears myself by the realization that he hadn't expected me to understand or have faith in him. It was evidently a new experience to have someone fight his battles for him. I told him, 'Anytime, buddy'. And he winked and said, 'Okay' before giving me my overdue punch and going off with William and a stick to play in the field. I never again saw him as openly emotional, but from then on there was an understanding between us – he knew that I knew he was okay, and I knew that he trusted me.

In the middle of August the inevitable happened.

I had just come back from what had turned into a two hour dog walk with Florin due to William having chased a deer to the other side of the forest. Florin had missed supper at the orphanage so I had brought him home for eggs and beans. At about half past six Moona and Fiona arrived, both looking pale, and told me that Blondu had just fallen from the roof. An ambulance was taking him to Dorohoi Hospital; they thought someone should follow him there and presumed that I would want to be that person. I remember little except feeling very numb and grabbing my jacket. Florin handed me the car keys and Guido, a volunteer mechanic from Luxembourg who tried to keep the worn out orphanage vehicles running, offered to come with me. I drove like a maniac to Dorohoi, trying to block out the images in my mind, trying to remember what Fiona had said about nothing being obviously broken. We reached the hospital and ran in, frantically opening doors to find him, screaming at nurses to tell us where he was. Eventually a doctor told us that the child from Yonashen had been sent on to Botoshani. They suspectened he had a broken spine, he said, and they didn't have the facilities to cope with that at Dorohoi.

I tore out to the car again, where Guido took the keys off me and insisted on driving. Even so we came within an inch of crashing into a light-less, reflector-less cart on the road to Botoshani, and I thanked God I hadn't been at the wheel. About ten miles from Botoshani we caught up with an ambulance and we followed it, convinced it must have Blondu inside it. When we reached the town, however, it turned the wrong way and I thought we must have made a mistake. But we followed it just in case, and a voice inside me suddenly panicked that the orphanage staff were perhaps taking the opportunity to give Blondu that electric shock treatment that they had been threatening for so long. At last the ambulance pulled up and I leapt out of the car; I saw Blondu through the now-opened side door, lying on a stretcher in the back, just conscious and groaning like a wounded animal.

'What's happening? Where are you taking him?'

'Oh, we're going to the children's hospital,' said the driver, as the man who had been in the passenger's seat said goodnight and walked off towards a nearby apartment block. 'I was just giving my friend a lift home.'

Luckily I wasn't in a state to reply to this. Instead I climbed into the ambulance beside Blondu and told the driver that I was coming with him to the hospital. Blondu recognized me and groaned even louder: he looked terrified and I tried to think of words to reassure him. The journey seemed to take hours and he winced at every bump, while I cursed Romanian roads and prayed that it wasn't causing irreparable damage to Blondu.

We reached the hospital and eventually found a doctor inside, watching television in the staff room on the second floor. He summoned two nurses who carried out the stretcher while I tried to keep hold of Blondu's hand. They managed to bump him into every doorway and wall on the way to the X-ray theatre, snapping at me to shut up whenever I told them to be more careful. They rolled him off on to the table and the doctor began prodding him, pronouncing his spine to be fine but saying that he probably had internal haemorrhaging, broken ribs and possibly a broken hip. They began taking X-rays, impervious to Blondu's screams as they straightened out his legs and held them down. His eyes didn't leave me, begging me to make them stop hurting him, and I felt like a traitor as I repeated words of reassurance while not being able to do anything to help him.

They dropped him on a stretcher again and banged it all the way upstairs to one of the wards where they hauled him on to an unmade bed, throwing some none-too-clean sheets and pyjamas at me and telling me to get him dressed. I was terrified of moving him but somehow pulled the sheet underneath him and the pyjama bottoms up his legs. Another nurse then came in with a terrifyingly thick needle and syringe and took a blood sample from his arm. She returned a few minutes later and proceeded to give him a series of shots in his hand and bottom. At each one Blondu screamed louder and then he started sobbing and clinging on to me. I begged her to stop; I didn't think he could take much more. I then started crying too, I think with relief more than anything, that he was alive and his back wasn't broken and he was still around to cling on to me.

The doctor came in with the X-rays and told me that his ribs were all right but he had a fractured hip – this wasn't serious though, and apparently would heal by itself. He said he wouldn't know about the haemorrhaging until he had the results of the blood tests so there was nothing he could do about that now. He invited Guido and me into the staff room, I thought so that he could give us more details but no, he just wanted to practise his English on us and find out if we thought there were any opportunities for him to find work in Britain. Whenever I mentioned Blondu he just said, 'Oh, don't worry about him, he'll be fine,' and began asking me what my favourite music was and how much did a doctor earn in Britain?

I returned to Blondu's bedside and tried to clean him up. He'd evidently been his usual muddy self before the accident and his recent injections had produced an incredible amount of blood that was now dried on his bottom, arm and face. I asked for some water, only to be told that there wasn't any. I suggested a towel and was given what looked like a well-used floor cloth, so in the end I used my T-shirt with spit on it and cleaned him up as well as I could.

Blondu finally fell asleep and Guido wrenched me away. We drove home feeling shattered but relieved, relatively sure that he was going to be all right, although my confidence in the medical opinion we had heard was not great. I returned to the hospital the next day with some of the other volunteers and we found Blondu pale but awake, obviously in pain but very much alive. There were still no results from his first blood test – it took 24 hours – but the doctor on duty told me they were treating the possible haemorrhaging as serious and already giving him drugs for it just in case.

The next day, the results came through and the doctors made plans for operating some time over the next few days. This depended on later blood tests which would show how well his body was coping with the injuries on its own. My persistent questioning of the doctors revealed that the operation would involve a blood transfusion. Once again I was thrown into total panic.

This came a week after my and Susan's visit to Baby Orphanage No 2 and our discovery that over half of the children there had been infected with the HIV virus by exposure in this very hospital. I grew almost hysterical at the thought of Blondu surviving his fall only to be given AIDS-infected blood, and I screamed at the doctors until they promised that they wouldn't operate without informing me first. I found out Blondu's blood group and cursed that it wasn't the same group as my own. Back at Yonashen though, I found that Evie's blood was the same group and she was happy to give blood, on the understandable condition that it was administered by Fiona. The doctors, of course, objected to my interference but finally agreed – probably just to shut me up.

In the end, thankfully, they never operated at all. His body managed to cope with the haemorrhaging remarkably well on its own; he was soon eating, his colour returned to his face, and in typical Blondu-style he was moving about much earlier than he should have been. By day four he was back to characteristic tricks. Informed of my arrival by others in the ward who had seen me drive up in the Land Rover from the window, he managed to hide under his bed, thus sending me on a wild goose chase round the building, screaming at doctors and nurses to tell me where they had taken him. I returned to his ward to find him sitting up in bed chortling with laughter – and I knew for sure that he was heading for a full recovery.

I was not popular amongst the medical staff, partly because of my frequent hysterical eruptions at any sign of possible danger to Blondu, but also because of the issue of bribes. The first open signs of hostility from the nurses came when I began bringing presents for Blondu – games for him to play, sweets and bottles of fruit juice. I was informed by the other mothers in the ward that I was meant to bring presents for the *staff*, not the children.

'But why?' I asked.

'Because otherwise he won't be fed, he won't be taken to the toilet, he won't be given medication.'

I was then treated to numerous accounts of what all of them were having to 'pay' for their children's medical treatment – chickens, pigs, maize, coffee, and often all their savings. They couldn't understand my reaction; to them doctors were powerful people and if you wanted help from one of them you had to pay. They seemed amazed that I should be so worked up about it. 'Surely you can afford it?' they said – and refused to believe that it wasn't the same in Britain.

In most areas of Romanian life I had long since recognized that to achieve anything we had to play the game, that our job was to help the children rather than attempt to change the huge problem of an immoral bureaucracy, and bribes on the whole were simply the oil that made the cogs of the system go round. But the principle of health care was too important and was the one area where I felt we had to make a stand. If the parents of the other children in the ward saw me giving presents to the staff, it would have legitimized the whole process. The Romanian Government was reaping huge benefits from its claim to the donor countries of the West that it had a system of free national health care from which to distribute and administer medical aid. If a doctor's salary was less than half that of a miner's, I reckoned that was a problem for the Government, not a shortfall for the patients to make up. If it was a recognized private system it wouldn't have been so bad, with established prices to pay for treatment, but it was worse than that – some had paid endless bribes but still had not received the health care they deserved because they simply didn't have the right connections. I thought back to Edit, the doctor I had met on my travels, and of how she had told me of having to play God in choosing whom to treat with her limited resources. Evidently many other doctors relished this role and were making a fortune out of it.

So I made my stand, for what it was worth, trying to ensure Blondu's proper care by threatening that if there was any sign of them not having done their jobs properly, I would report them to my friend the Health Minister in Bucharest and get them sacked. I could only hope that Blondu didn't suffer too much for this. I relied largely on the other mothers who were almost permanently in the ward to ensure that Blondu was given food at mealtimes and taken to the toilet regularly.

There was also a noticeable sense of incredulity among the hospital staff, verging on disgust, that anyone should be paying so much attention and creating so much fuss about a deaf and dumb child from an orphanage. One day I was visiting with Florin when an Italian couple came round the wards with presents for all the children. I heard them ask the nurse accompanying them as to what was wrong with Blondu, presuming of course that I was just another of the Romanian mothers sitting by their children. In reply the nurse didn't even mention Blondu's fall, his broken hip or the haemorrhaging.

'Oh, he's an irrecuperable. He has no intelligence at all, there's nothing in his head. The one next to him, too,' she said, pointing to Florin, 'although he perhaps has a chance of improving, but the blond one, no, there's no hope for him.'

This was the first time I'd actually heard the word

'*irecuperabil*' being spoken – before I'd just seen it written in the children's medical papers – and it rendered me practically speechless. I managed to inform the Italian couple that the form of Blondu's handicap was in fact deafness, that both children were highly intelligent and capable, and that their greatest problems arose from the fact that they had spent most of their lives stuck in an orphanage resembling a concentration camp. At this the nurse stalked off in a huff, and Blondu and Florin did their Oliver Twist acts, managing to relieve the Italians of all the remaining sweets and toys in their bag.

Blondu's spell in hospital revealed to me the depth of affection between him and many of the care workers at Yonashen, however. The beatings he received from some had hidden the fact that by others he was loved; on most evenings I drove care staff into Botoshani to see him, laden with cakes and doughnuts they had made for him. He in return was overjoyed to see them, hugging and kissing them. Henry made a huge 'Get Well' card for him that was signed by everyone from Mitica to the boilerman, and Blondu stuck it on the wall by his bed with great pride and aplomb. It made me realize that, terrible place though it was for a child to grow up in, Yonashen was the only home that Blondu knew – and to him that's what it was, *home*, full of the people he knew and loved. When the time came finally for him to leave hospital, he arrived back at Yonashen a returning hero, thrilled to see everyone and everything. He did the rounds of the building, shaking hands and hugging all he met, proudly showing off his limp and refusing to go to bed.

Blondu hadn't been out of hospital a week when I suddenly fell ill myself. It started off as something like flu; I had a high fever and aching limbs, so I retired to bed in my little house in the village in an attempt to sweat it out. I worsened my condition considerably by reading *Silence of the Lambs*, working myself into such a state of terror that I even had to take William with me to the bottom of the garden whenever I needed the loo, so convinced was I that a psychopath was about to leap on me.

After about five days I began getting terrible headaches, I couldn't stand the light and I grew delirious. When Guido found me one night rolling round in my garden trying to bury my head in the ground to stop the pain, I realized things might be getting serious. Fiona was worried that I might have meningitis and said that if I wasn't any better the next day I must fly home. I remembered the trauma involved in any flight from Bucharest airport and decided I would rather just curl up and die in my nice safe bed. For the first time I experienced the fear of being in a country without a system of health care worthy of the name. Close to convincing myself that I was about to die in this God-forsaken corner of Moldavia, I was determined not to let anyone take me to hospital in Botoshani. I remember making Fiona promise that, if it became so bad that they did, she would stay with me. I thanked God that Fiona was about; she was marvellous, visiting me regularly even though she had no medicines that could help me, and did much to stop me from panicking when I felt that my brain was exploding.

Fortunately I improved without treatment and after another few days was up on my feet again. I was a stone lighter and I realized that much of my oomph, the drive that we all needed to fight Yonashen's battles day after day, was gone. It was now approaching the end of August and I was meant to be back in England soon. My book was being launched and I was under strict orders to be back in time. The Land Rover was also desperately in need of repairs and I knew I'd soon be immobilized if I didn't take it back before anything else went wrong. So reluctantly I began preparing for the journey home; I planned to return to Yonashen in a month's time, thence to set off on my donkey travels once more, but nevertheless the thought of saying goodbye to the kids filled me with dread.

The family who had looked after Hannibal for me over the summer agreed to keep him whilst I was away, but the dogs had to come back with me as far as France. I couldn't plonk them on a volunteer for so long and, although many had said they would gladly have them, I knew that leaving them with a villager would mean them being kept on a short chain outside all day. I reckoned kennels in France would be kinder, and I planned to spend some time in France anyway, visiting my sister.

The last few days were chaotic, due to a series of mechanical failures which left me in serious doubt as to whether the Land Rover would make it back to England, and also because of a coup in the Soviet Union. The latter threw the Romanians into total panic; the first we heard of it was that the tanks were coming. The changes in Eastern Europe had been entirely dependent upon Gorbachev's *perestroika*, and the Romanians were sure that if right-wing communists returned to power in Moscow then Romania would be back to satellite status immediately. We were less than 40 miles from the Soviet border and you could almost feel the tension in the air. We sat in the volunteers' room round my short-wave radio trying to pick up the World Service and were almost disappointed to learn that Romania was the last thing on anyone's mind the other side of the border. Gorbachev was released and the crisis died down as quickly as it had blown up, but it revealed the level of paranoia in most Romanian minds regarding the Russian threat. Any suggestion that the Soviet Union had far too many problems of its own to have the time or the inclination to invade Romania produced the usual patriotic fervour – 'And why wouldn't they want to invade us? We are a great country, a rich country, we were always the jewel in the Communist crown. Of *course* they'd want to invade us.'

On the day of Gorbachev's reappearance the canvas cover was stolen from the Land Rover. No one in the village knew anything about it, naturally, but when I returned to Yonashen a month later I was interested to see a new fashion in canvas overcoats in the area, in a distinctly familiar shade of blue. We managed to stick on a plastic replacement with tarred roofing tape, but I didn't hold out much hope that it would survive for long. The Land Rover was also billowing out vast amounts of black smoke, which I became convinced would get us arrested as soon as we entered Austria.

The final morning of departure was terrible. I had tried to explain to Blondu that I was leaving and would be coming back again, but conveying a sense of time and the future to a deaf child is almost impossible and he didn't realize what was happening until he saw the Land Rover packed up and ready outside the gate. He made it a million times harder by climbing in, pleading with me to let him come too, so that I had to carry him out as I tried desperately, and not very successfully, not to cry. He started sobbing and wouldn't let go of me. Moona had to pull him from me, and I collapsed into a pool of tears in the passenger seat as Evie drove us away down the track to Virfu Cimpului.

Chapter 9

Calm Before the Storm

Three days later we were back in England, having driven non-stop with just a four-hour break in Germany when the Land Rover's lights failed on the autobahn. I left the dogs at a boarding kennels in Le Havre – yet more tearful goodbyes – and, back in London, slept for nearly two days before emerging to face family and friends.

The reality of Western life came to me as a total culture shock, and I found myself continuously ringing Evie to make sure that I wasn't alone in feeling so out of touch. London was nothing like the city I had left – it had never been so clean, and before, it seemed, there had not been such amazingly wonderful things in the shops. Even going to a supermarket proved to be a mind-boggling experience, as I found myself totally incapable of making any decisions about what to buy. When shopping with a friend, who asked me to choose something for supper, I headed for the ready-prepared meals section: the friend found me still standing there 15 minutes later, staring at the shelves with my mouth wide open.

During the launch of my book I felt as though I were going mad. I had to forget Romania, forget Yonashen and the kids, and make out as if I'd just returned from my previous travels in Italy. I had to re-read my own book to remind myself what had happened in what felt like another life. I put on my jolly girl adventurer's face and talked on local radio and television about donkeys and mad Italians, waiting for the last two minutes of the interview when, if I was lucky, I was asked, 'And you've been doing something rather extraordinary lately, haven't you, Sophie?' I usually never got beyond, 'Yes, John, I've been in Romania working at an . . .' before I was cut off by the credits. Romania, it seemed, was old news. Apart from the loyal *Westmorland Gazette*, my local paper at home, nobody even pretended to be remotely interested in Yonashen. The orphanages 'happened' in 1990, apparently, and there was no more mileage to be had from them.

At the other end of the scale many friends greeted me as some kind of returning saint, which I found even more difficult to handle, and which only increased my growing sense of guilt whenever I spoke of Yonashen. I couldn't stop thinking of all the things I could and should have done whilst I was there. Whenever I ate a meal I pictured the volunteers living off instant mash and cold beans and the kids eating their pork fat stew (I wolfed down food as if I was eating on behalf of them all, soon putting back all the weight I'd lost, and more).

My mind played cruel tricks on me, never letting me forget. Whenever I was somewhere nice I kept imagining Blondu and Florin with me, thinking how much they would love the shops, the buses, the trains, the fast food . . . When I went up to the Lake District to stay with my parents and took a boat out on Lake Windermere I thought of how much fun it would be to teach them to sail. It kept haunting me, the knowledge that they would never experience all these things that I had always taken for granted.

I wasn't very good company for the majority of my friends who didn't share my new-found belief that British society was something precious and wonderful, to be marvelled at and preserved at all costs. The economic depression in Britain was worsening but the understandable pub remarks concerning the wickedness of the Tory Government would have me standing on my stool yelling, 'So you think life's tough, huh? I'll show you tough, I'll show you wicked', etc., etc.

My plans changed once again. I decided to scrap my travels altogether and return to Yonashen to do all that I should have done before. I promised my Mum and my agent that I'd be back for Christmas to start the writing that was meant to be my reason for going to Romania in the first place, but I felt a burning need to do more for Yonashen, to really make the contribution that my friends seemed to be crediting me with. I knew I couldn't bring the kids home but nor was I ready to just write them off as an interesting episode of my life.

I went over to France to give the dogs a break from kennels and to visit my sister, Emu, in Paris. She was between jobs and wasn't due to start the next one till after Christmas. Sipping beer at a Parisian street cafe, I suddenly found myself asking her whether she'd come out to Romania with me, and with a spur of the moment decision she said 'yes'. I realized what an asset she would be to Yonashen; she had worked a great deal with handicapped children. But I think more than that I wanted someone amongst my family and friends to understand what it was really like out there. I had experienced something important that was impossible to share. My sister and I are very close, and I felt a huge surge of relief that I'd be able to talk to her about it all when the time finally came for me to leave for good.

Thus in October I drove back in the much repaired but still heavily smoking Land Rover. The weather in Romania was still surprisingly mild, although the trees were leafless and everything looked muddy and grey compared to the summer greenery I had left behind. It felt good to be back, and I was given what felt like a hero's welcome from the Yonashen children. Hannibal looked extremely fat and well and was suitably disgusted to see me; Florin bowled me over by giving me a great smacker of a kiss and Blondu leapt all over me, although both reserved the most rapturous welcome for the dogs. It felt good to see everyone, although amongst the volunteers there were many new faces which threw me. There was a Londoner called Mary who was doing wonders apparently sorting through the chaos of our charity accounts; and a nurse of twenty-five from Edinburgh called Maureen who was working in *Triaj*. These two were living in the house of the family in the village who were looking after Hannibal for me, and when I met them told me hilarious stories of the way my donkey would attack them on their evening dashes over to the loo shed in the yard. There was a good-looking blond chap of about the same age called Andrew, also from Edinburgh, on to whom Silvio had latched as if he'd found a long lost brother. Andrew always seemed to be at the table in the volunteers' room engrossed in complicated charts; I was told that he was in charge of transport, which seemed a most peculiar position until I discovered that the much talked of Toyotas had arrived. The Irish groups had bought and driven out a Toyota four wheel drive Hilux and a Hiace minibus; they were objects of marvel to us all, and my faithful old Land Rover that had driven to the rescue so often during the summer was suddenly no longer in constant demand.

I was soon busy again, organizing bulk buys of apples, pears, cabbages and potatoes to put into storage for the winter, and trying to solve the food crisis brought on by the expected October price rises. The cost of most state supplied goods had doubled while the children's food allowance had increased to just 96 *lei* (about 25 pence; with Romania's high rate of inflation, about the same value as the previous allowance of 76 *lei*). Predictably Mitica and Lenutsa wanted to cut out my dairy produce and vegetables rather than the biscuits and fat that I wanted rid of; the familiar arguments began and I was soon feeling at home.

Moona set Jon and me to work on plans for a bakery in the village. The nearest supply of bread was currently in Buchecha and thus inaccessible to most of the villagers. It was brought to the orphanage by horse and cart every other day, but the quality was appalling – Fiona had taken a sample home for tests and discovered that in Britain it would not even be fit for animal consumption. We had been donated a working set of bakery equipment, which Mike faithfully brought out in three articulated lorry loads; there was a dilapidated building in the village which had once been a bakery, and somehow we had to put the two together and try to start making bread.

Emu, meanwhile, began working on the diet of the volunteers. The latter had been a constant source of contention between myself and Moona in the summer; he thought we should all eat from the orphanage kitchen, while I insisted that the children's food should be just that, for the children, and I knew full well that the kitchen staff made extra little tit-bits for Moona while they were content to send the usual fatty slop along to *Triaj*. Most of the volunteers lived off an arbitrary selection of supplies sent out on aid trucks – Smash and tinned sardines, instant soups and the odd box of cornflakes, eaten in the volunteers' room whenever they had a break. In the summer I had tried to make an effort to take other volunteers into Botoshani or Suchava for a square meal at a restaurant as often as possible. Many didn't have the funds to afford this themselves, and I always felt it was wrong that people who were being paid nothing were not at least supplied with a decent meal to keep them going.

Emu, a trained cook, began creating surprisingly delicious concoctions on the two electric rings in the volunteers' room, mixing aid supplies with what was available in the Botoshani markets bought from charity funds. For the first time we all sat down for proper lunches and suppers, and the volunteers' room was suddenly organized and tidy. Emu felt increasingly frustrated that she wasn't doing 'proper' work, as she put it, and in any free time she had she went into the Sections to help out, and did much to raise volunteer morale and settled into Yonashen life much more quickly than I had.

Within a week of our arrival the weather suddenly changed and I thanked God that I had abandoned my travel plans. The temperatures plummeted and the first snows came, transforming the roads into lethal ice rinks and producing a fuel crisis at the orphanage. Two aid trucks on their way out from Dublin got stuck coming through the mountains; Moona drove out to the rescue in the Toyota and finally they arrived, bringing amongst all the more important supplies, plus a most welcome box of anoraks and thick coats for us all.

The Irish also had some supplies for Podriga, the adult institution. Some aid workers had been there during the summer but had inexplicably left. With some of the other Yonashen volunteers I decided to visit it, out of a kind of morbid curiosity as to what kind of place the kids would go to when they grew up. I still wish that I hadn't.

From the outside it was a formidable looking building, a nobleman's residence like Yonashen but much more like the setting for a horror film, with two pointed towers, outside balconies and round stone stairways. Huge black crows almost covered the roof, and as we drove closer we noticed the collapsing pillars, the crumbling plasterwork, the smashed windows. Broken guttering hung down on to rotting brickwork and roof tiles lay smashed on the ground. A rusty nameplate above the front entrance told us this was 'PODRIGA, Psychiatric Section of Saveni Hospital'.

Apart from the cold, it did not seem too bad inside. There was no one about, which seemed strange after the constant activity at Yonashen, but the front rooms looked clean and the neat rows of beds implied a decent level of care. A terrible smell came from the toilet area, but after nearly a year in the country I was becoming accustomed to these standards of hygiene.

We wandered outside and saw a stone staircase leading down to the basement. As we descended and the stench hit us, my hand instinctively covered my mouth and nostrils, and I had a violent urge to run back up. I knew I wasn't going to like what I found down there. We stood for a while at the bottom letting our eyes adjust to the darkness, and then noticed a narrow corridor leading off to the left towards the sound of voices.

The room was full of people; from the pathetic light of the single bulb it was impossible to say exactly how many, but I guessed about sixty. It was warm, which explained why they were there; many were naked, or almost so. Their heads were shaved and they were rocking, most of them silently, to and fro, on thin wooden benches alongside filthy tables. The woodburning stove in the corner was covered with bodies; two were squashed into the tiny gap between the stove and the wall.

I suddenly felt enormous and very aware of my two thick jumpers and down jacket. Some of the men looked like Auschwitz victims, their rounded spines seemingly trying to hide their protruding ribs and hollow stomachs. Many were covered in sores, which they scratched at incessantly, whilst others picked at lice in their pubic hair. Some turned towards us, holding out their hands and asking for clothes or food, but most just continued staring straight ahead and rocking, back and forth, back and forth.

The room was flooded, I presumed by water until I saw a broken pipe leading from the floor above, dripping what smelt like human excrement. The brown walls were covered in condensation and the air was filled with a foul-smelling smoke. There was constant coughing and wheezing, as if they were all being slowly suffocated, but still someone screamed at us to shut the door, for we were letting in the cold.

In a tiny adjoining room two old ladies were scrubbing dishes in an iron cauldron. A man entered and began washing coal dust from his body in the same water. One of the women began crying, telling me she'd been beaten up that morning, and as I offered sympathy she kissed me and clung on to me as though she would never let me go.

Outside again, we walked to a long barn-like building a hundred yards from the main house. This was called the Pavilion. We entered a room that suddenly made the basement we had just witnessed seem almost decent. There were kids here, children who looked no older than twelve, crouching naked on a wooden bench, urinating directly on to the floor as we approached them. I held out my arms to one of them and he sprang away in fear, leaping on to a bed where three emaciated bodies lay under a sodden blanket. I turned back to the others; one was rubbing what looked like faeces into his hair. A little girl was hitting the side of her head. As I tried to distract her attention to stop her, showing her my pen, I realized that she must hit her head constantly for only half her ear was left.

We backed out and tried a door on the other side of the building. Beds with stinking black mattresses were crammed into every space. An old man lay in one and we moved over to him, wondering why he wasn't in the warmer room next door with the others. He was utterly still and Maureen suddenly reached for his pulse.

He was dead.

The journey back to Yonashen was made in complete silence. As I got out of the minibus Blondu rushed towards me and I clung on to him, forgetting I was meant to be angry with him for hurling a stone at me when

I'd left without him. I buried my face into his neck and found that I couldn't stop sobbing. That place was his future. I thought of him there and I couldn't bear it.

SECTION III

Podriga

Chapter 10

Fighting the System

Andrew, the blond Scottish chap who had arrived at Yonashen at the end of August just after I'd left for England, proved to be the driving force behind the decision that something must be done about Podriga. He called a meeting the next day to inform the other volunteers of what we had found and I sat on the phone with him all afternoon ringing the larger charities based in Bucharest in the hope that they might want to send a team up. However, they all claimed to be up to their ears in their own projects, especially with winter approaching, and many said that because Podriga was an adult institution, it was out of their reach – their funds had been raised specifically for children. The Romanian Relief Fund in London said they had an aid truck coming out in three weeks' time and if we established a volunteer presence at Podriga they'd send some basic supplies to us. But we were soon painfully aware that no one else was going to take it on and do the donkey work.

None of us who had seen it could forget, and a kind of depression set in amongst us regarding what we were doing at Yonashen. What was the point in working so hard and spending so much money on building a decent environment for the children if at the end of the day they were to be thrown back into the rags and filth of somewhere like Podriga? It would have been kinder never to have come at all. Setting up the bakery in the village seemed trivial and meaningless. My heart was no longer in it and I found myself drawn more and more to Andrew's meetings as he tried to form a group of volunteers to move to Podriga as soon as possible. There were over twenty of us at Yonashen and it was obvious that some of us could be spared without causing any great loss to the kids – and I grew more and more aware that I was one of them.

I kept slapping myself on the wrists and trying to stop myself. I had to go home in December and the last thing I needed was to become yet more involved in Romania. But I knew that a team at Podriga would find life extremely hard without transport and someone who could speak Romanian. Of the four Romanian-speakers amongst the volunteers at Yonashen, Moona and Fiona were indispensable and Jon could not move since he also worked at another small orphanage near Yonashen. That left me, and I had the Land Rover which was no longer really needed at Yonashen. It began to seem more and more stupid *not* to go and help out at Podriga. I convinced myself that it would just be for six weeks, until Christmas, to help get things started until the others picked up Romanian and a vehicle was donated. I told Andrew to add my name to his list.

Before any definite plans could be made we had to find out if we'd even be *allowed* to work at Podriga. No one knew for sure what had happened to the two British volunteers who had been there the previous spring. We contacted FARA, the charity they had worked under, and were informed that their supplies had been constantly stolen and they had been badly beaten up in a fight apparently inspired by Podriga's management. FARA told us that, while wanting to help the Podriga residents, they had made a decision to give nothing more unless Podriga was transferred from the authority of the Ministry of Health to that of the Secretariat for the Handicapped, the former being apparently too corrupt to work with. We began to realize we could be treading through a minefield.

Unlike Yonashen, Podriga did not have its own director. It came under the management of the hospital in the nearby town of Saveni, of which Podriga was officially the 'psychiatric section'. We made an appointment to see Dr Apostol, the director of Saveni Hospital, and Fiona accompanied Andrew and me on our quest for permission to work at Podriga. We were kept waiting in his well-padded office for a good half hour before finally meeting a large, bulbous-faced man of about sixty, who soon revealed an enormous dislike of the British. He lectured us for almost an hour on what amounted to, in his opinion, British war crimes against Romania during the Second World War – on how the British relentlessly bombed civilian targets, how the Romanian resistance were given no help at all and how finally, in the crime of all crimes at Yalta in 1944, half of Moldavia was given away to the Russians.

We apologized profusely, grateful at least that we weren't American for he loathed Eisenhower even more than Churchill. He gradually moved on to more contemporary topics, but his theme was the same – that the Western nations think they can just waltz into Romania and tell the Romanians what is good for them. Regarding aid, almost all of the medicines and equipment he had been sent and was expected to be grateful for was out of date or broken. What kind of insult was this, he asked? The drugs weren't good enough for Westerners, but they were quite all right for second class human beings such as Romanians, were they? Well he wasn't going to take it, he told us. He was not going to be grateful for such contemptuous gestures, and he was certainly not going to beg foreigners for help. Romania was a great nation and it did not need others to tell it how to run its affairs and look after its own.

We kept trying to steer the conversation back to Podriga.

Dr Apostol told us that endless foreign organizations had come to him since the revolution saying they wanted to help, but none had followed it through and come up with the goods. We found ourselves apologizing for all of them, too, relying on Yonashen as our trump card, our proof that we were people who would stick to our promises. When he finally gave us the go-ahead, we were astonished – we had convinced ourselves that we would have to go higher before he would agree to let us into Podriga. But we could have a go, he said. He clearly didn't expect any results and he told us he was certainly not going to pretend to be grateful for our help, but if we wanted to try he would not stop us.

He introduced us to a shifty-looking man called Marcan, the 'administrative director' of Saveni Hospital who was apparently responsible for the day-to-day running of Podriga, and we arranged to have a meeting with him in three days' time. Meanwhile we set about the most immediate problem – accommodation for a volunteer team. The easiest option would be to ask around the village of Podriga for lodging with Romanian families, but we all felt that, at the beginning at least, we needed to be together and we wanted a safe place to store supplies, so we approached the mayor of Saveni to see about the possibility of renting an apartment in the town.

The mayor was young, good-looking and friendly – in fact so unlike the usual mould of Romanian officials that it was hard to take him seriously at first. He proved to be one of our greatest allies in Saveni, however. Though his jurisdiction did not reach beyond the town boundaries and Podriga was not officially his responsibility, I was soon turning to him with all manner of problems. In that first meeting he told us there was a waiting list for accommodation in the town, but he would put us to the top of the queue and meanwhile he would arrange for us to stay in Saveni's hotel. 'Hotel' is probably too grand a word. The rooms we were shown had mould growing over the walls, shredded curtains, stained bedcovers and bathrooms inch-deep in grime, but the manager agreed to charge us just 100 *lei* (25 pence) a night and said it was no problem bringing the dogs.

A few days later Andrew and I drove over for the arranged meeting with Marcan. We met him in his office at the hospital; a good fire was burning and we were brought coffee. He was a pointy-featured man of about fifty; he wore a Communist style black leather belted jacket with an open shirt and jumper beneath. His face was set in a permanent semi-snarl, and he did not seem at all pleased to see us. With him was the hospital accountant, a younger man with a round smiling face named Alexandrovich, whom we both instantly felt was smarmy. We sat down after making our introductions, and tried to begin a friendly discussion of Podriga's problems.

They had not come for a friendly discussion, however. Marcan immediately set about giving us a series of demands, which he wrote down as a list on a sheet of paper in front of us, while beside him Alexandrovich smiled and nodded approval. It was a shopping list – 'new well, US$10,000', 'industrial laundry, US$5,000', 'electric central heating system, US$20,000', etc., etc. – almost a whole page full.

I didn't know whether to laugh or cry. On the one hand I kept thinking of the money we had – a loan of 150 pounds from the Yonashen kitty, and 2,000 dollars sent over from my mother – but then I realized that even if we had millions, nothing would induce me to hand any of it over to these two. Whenever we tried to bring up one of the items on their list and talk about the problems behind it, Marcan would snap back that they didn't believe we had the money and we were just wasting their valuable time. *They* had been in charge of Podriga for years, they said, so of course they knew what was needed – they didn't need foreigners to tell them, and either we wanted to help or we didn't.

Totally against the idea of our actually moving to Podriga to work, they said that the problems were purely financial ones, and all we had to do was sign the cheques. We had no business disturbing the Podriga patients in their everyday lives, Marcan warned – some of them are seriously mentally ill, you know, and we could do great damage if we upset their routine. There are qualified medical assistants caring for them – who were we?

I should have laughed at them, but there was something about their manner that I found very threatening. Perhaps it was the simple knowledge on both sides of the table that they had great power over what we would be able to do at Podriga. We would always have to seek their permission, never the other way round. They would never come begging to us, for it was already evident that they didn't really give a damn whether Podriga got its shopping list or not; and as Marcan sneered across at me, perhaps he was already imagining all the times we'd go begging to him over the years to come.

Dr Apostol had agreed to a team of five of us up at Podriga, and five was all that he, Marcan, wanted – so we weren't to bring in great hordes of colleagues as soon as his back was turned. We must seek permission for any changes we wanted to make, and we were to tell him of any problems we encountered. Meanwhile, he would like to meet our boss so that he could make his financial requests to someone with more authority than us.

We told them that we planned to start at Podriga the next Monday, and then we left. I felt full of conflicting emotions – a sense of being a fraud, because we had no money; that we were just a bunch of well-meaning amateurs who perhaps could do very little to really help the Podriga residents. Yet at the same time Marcan and Alexandrovich had convinced me that Podriga's problems were *not* purely financial. We had a snoop around Saveni Hospital, and while it was hardly up to model Western standards, it seemed so next to Podriga. It was warm and clean, the walls were freshly painted; the rooms were too tightly packed with beds, but they were made up with crisp sheets and blankets and there were flowers on the table. Podriga was officially part of this same hospital, but the difference in standards made them worlds apart. The problem, I felt sure, was one of priorities – the changing of which was going to be a great deal harder than the simple raising of cash.

On Sunday, 10 November we made the move over to Saveni, arriving in the late afternoon blue with cold after the one and a half hour journey in the Land Rover. There was Andrew, main instigator of the move, with Smecky, the little white puppy dumped at Yonashen a month previously whom no one had been able to destroy and whom Andrew had taken in. There was Colette Hughes plus guitar, for once fairly subdued. There was Maureen, the nurse from Edinburgh who had been working in *Triaj* for the past two months, and Aileen, a quiet, pretty girl from Aberdeen who'd been working in the Front Section throughout the summer but whom I had never really got to know. With me were William and Georgie, not looking too keen about resuming their travels once more. Jon drove over in the Yonashen minibus, filled with some very basic supplies; its windows were smashed during the hour Jon left it parked in Saveni, and we all felt a great sense of foreboding.

None of us had been happy to leave Yonashen. Blondu had seen my packed bags and presumed I was off back to England again so there had been tears at the gate. We therefore weren't in the best of moods for enjoying the surprise four-course meal that the mayor had organized in our honour at Saveni's one and only restaurant on Sunday evening. It was a chance for me to find out all I could about the area from the mayor and his deputy, but the others sat in polite silence. From their faces I knew what they were thinking, because I had been feeling the same sense of panic for days. What the hell were we doing? How much of our lives were we signing away in an attempt to help those people at Podriga? None of us had a clue what lay ahead; we knew only that we were going to have to tread very carefully, and I for one was scared as hell.

Our first week was immensely frustrating. It was a week of learning, of trying to find out who was responsible for what, and thus how we could even start to change things, but at the same time we felt that all we really wanted to do was start scrubbing and clearing the place up.

We slowly introduced ourselves to the Podriga staff and residents. It was so like a prison that it was difficult not to call them inmates; the staff referred to them as the '*bolnavi*', the sick ones, but we decided on 'residents' in an attempt to improve their status nominally at least. We counted 87, 45 of them men and 42 women, although these numbers were soon to go up.

The barn-like building where we'd found the dead man on our first visit was referred to by both staff and residents as the 'Pavilion'. It was an unmitigated hell-hole, full of the most disturbed residents whom the staff wanted to keep out of sight and out of mind. Thirty of them slept in the freezing cold room to the right of the entrance, on dilapidated iron beds with sodden, rotten mattresses and filthy, damp blankets. Their days were spent huddled round the stove in the adjoining room, with fights breaking out every hour between the more violent adults, while the kids sat on their bench in the corner, moving only to get out of the line of fire or to pounce on to the food that care workers brought over twice a day from the kitchen. Four 'children' in the Pavilion plus two more in the main building, the staff insisted, were all over eighteen. None were over four feet tall or weighed above five stone. They had apparently arrived the previous year from the orphanage at Stefanesti, a town to the east of Botoshani where I knew a French group had made great improvements. The shock they must have suffered when they arrived at Podriga was beyond my imagination. The children never spoke and continued to shrink from our efforts at communication, terrified of these strangers who appeared so interested in them.

The main building proved to be a warren of winding stone stairways, hidden rooms and locked doors. Up at the top we found a large dark attic used for drying laundry, storing onions and housing a sizeable family of rats. Below this, in the main upper storey, were four large perishingly cold bedrooms. Three of these were kept locked for most of the day, their occupants prevented from seeing any more of the outside walls than their limited views from the barred windows. The toilet area consisted of a doorless room with two six-inch diameter holes at the far end of a stone floor, and a drain in the middle. The privies had grids cemented over them, apparently to stop large objects being thrown down the pipes, but which resulted in piles of excrement being frozen solid to the wire. Many residents had evidently not dared venture all the way to the gridded holes and piles of faeces were dotted over the floor. The whole place stank and the walls were covered in shit and grime. Part of the ceiling had collapsed over one of the holes, revealing rotting beams and sodden reed filling.

The toilet arrangements were the same on the ground floor, but the conditions were even worse – the drain from the upper floor emptied straight out from the ceiling in a crusty brown funnel of raw sewage that must have once been part of a pipe. Slop cascaded over the whole toilet area whenever someone upstairs swept up the mess on that floor into the drain. The hell was made even worse by the equivalent drain in this floor being blocked, producing a great pool of floating faeces through which the residents had to wade to reach the toilets.

Downstairs in the basement we discovered that the flooding was caused by a large hole in the main sewage outlet pipe into which fed all the upstairs toilets and drains. Repairs had been attempted with plaster, pieces of wood and strips of cloth, through which a relentless thick brown trickle poured on to the floor of the small washroom next to the 'dining room' where the residents of the main building spent their days.

On the ground floor the rickety old wooden door that constituted the main entrance opened into a large, dark hall. It must have once been rather grand; a wide stone staircase led the wind howling up to the landing. Three doors on the right hand side led to the smarter bedrooms that had impressed me on my first visit; here were permitted to live those residents who did not wet their beds, who did not scream too much, who did not break their windows. To the left of a hall a corridor led past the toilet area to a small staff room. It contained a desk, two chairs, a bed, and an empty glass medical cabinet. It also contained most of the staff on duty, for here was Podriga's third functioning stove, red hot with a neat pile of firewood beside it. A tape recorder was plugged into the only socket in the whole building, blaring out Romanian folk music, and a kettle was permanently brewing up coffee. The staff seldom appeared to venture out at all from their warm bolthole, and at times the temperature elsewhere in the building made it hard to blame them.

Over the first week we went out of our way to befriend them and slowly I worked out the staffing set-up. The man described by all at Podriga as 'the chief' was the head of the four medical assistants, a man called Domnul Purice, which translates as 'Mr Headlice', and which proved to be an apt description. We discovered that he had two private store rooms which he kept under lock and key and he would not even describe the contents, let alone allow us in to see them. He also had a small sitting room of his own, complete with a fridge, an electric fire and a colour television, all of which, the residents told us, had been donated to Podriga by foreign aid groups. Headlice himself was a shrew-like little man with red hair and shifty pale eyes, always dressed in a tall black sheepskin hat and a regulation hospital dressing gown. From the start he was hostile, and a few days after our arrival he began disappearing as soon as we arrived in the morning.

The effective head of the workforce was one of the other medical assistants, a grossly fat woman named Marishika. She had dark hair and large brown eyes and could look quite friendly when she smiled, but as she stormed around the building shrieking orders at both staff and residents she was terrifying. She was always the warmest towards us, however, even if not in the way we would have wished – she was forever inviting us into the staff room for cups of coffee and swigs of *tsuica* that she kept in a drawer of a large wooden desk by the window.

There were two more medical assistants. It was hard to determine the meaning of 'medical assistant', but on the whole it seemed to be what we would call a nurse (a Romanian '*infirmiere*', or nurse, receives no training whatsoever). One of the medical assistants was an extremely smart woman called Anna. She always arrived dressed up to the nines in full make-up, high-heeled boots and expensive-looking hats; the other was Marishika's twin Gica, who was almost as fat as her sister but with much less charisma. They claimed to work eight-hour shifts, but we soon discovered that tardiness of buses and endless crises at home always reduced it to about six – not that it made much difference. They arrived at work, went straight to the staff room, made a cup of coffee, put their favourite tape into the machine, and generally they would stay there until the end of their shift, usually only venturing out to entice one of us in to join them. There were always piles of paperwork on the desk that occasionally they busied themselves with, but they certainly never did anything that would entail getting their hands dirty.

The work was left to the unqualified peasant women who made up the 'care' staff. There were four on duty each morning, and either one or two in the afternoon. I could see why most gave up before they'd even started – their task, to keep the place clean and tidy as well as care for the residents, was effectively impossible. They were given no soap or disinfectant, no mops, no scrubbing brushes, and my heart went out to them. The nicest of them, a small woman in her forties with soft brown eyes and hair who must have once been extremely pretty, started crying when we talked to her in one of the icy turret bedrooms upstairs. She was called Sandina, and I'd found her earlier trying to unblock the drain of the ground-floor toilets with her bare hands. As we tried to comfort her, she kept saying over and over how ashamed she felt.

'You wander round looking at the dilapidated buildings and the neglected residents,' she said, 'and you think that we are evil, that we have done this to them. You think that we don't care, that we are happy to let them live like this. You must think that I am a monster.'

She was sobbing and we tried to reassure her that we didn't blame her, that we knew how great the problems were and that she could never have changed things single-handed. She began to tell us about how much worse the situation had become since the revolution. Before December 1989, repairs had been made every year, things had been fixed, albeit badly, when they were broken, clothes had arrived for the residents – but since then, there had been nothing. The workforce had been reduced and the place was rapidly falling to pieces around them. She begged us to stay and help them, to do something before it was too late.

Others amongst the staff were wary at first, some like Headlice were surly and stayed out of our way, but most grew friendly over those first couple of weeks. In the main we just felt very sorry for them – it wasn't till later that we realized they had seen 'POTENTIAL GOLDMINE' written all over our naïve faces.

It proved much harder to get to know the residents. They were simply not used to talking and many seemed to have forgotten the art of communication. Even learning their names was a problem. When we asked them, most would just stare silently back at us. We queried the care workers instead, not realizing that very few of the staff knew the names of more than a handful of the residents. Too embarrassed to admit as much, they would confidently announce the first name that came into their head. This resulted in many confused arguments back in our hotel room:

'The one in the Pavilion with the squint and the big nose – he's *definitely* called Simon.'

'No, he's not, I heard Marishika call him Ion.'

'Well, the one who responded when I called her Maria was calling him Cosmin.'

Amongst those residents who had come to Podriga from Yonashen was one of the most charming men I've ever met, who fast became a favourite to all of us. His name was Mitica and he had cerebral palsy. His limbs were tightened and twisted by the muscle spasms characteristic of the disorder, yet somehow he managed to move around with impressive speed on his hands and knees. He was thrilled when he learnt that we'd come from Yonashen, quizzing us relentlessly about his former friends – how were Pedro and Mushat, Ivan and Stefan? He was always incredibly polite and gentlemanly, finding a chair for me when I came to his room to speak to him, addressing me always with the formal '*dumneavoastra*' rather than '*tu*' and generally perplexing me as to where on earth he could have learnt such manners.

Most, though, were not so receptive. As we tried over

that first week to just sit and talk to them all, we realized that many were locked into worlds of their own, surrounded by barriers they did not want us to break down. When we chatted to them about who we were and how we planned to be around for a while, they would often just stare deep into our eyes, as if searching in their minds for a memory of us that wasn't there. Others went off into rambling monologues, telling me of people and places from their past, and some would suddenly give great bursts of affection, hugging and kissing us before settling back just as quickly into their rocking silence on the dining room bench. The little old lady who had been crying in the washroom on our first visit, we discovered, was almost always crying. She worked like a slave, forever mopping up the dining room floor with a stinking old cloth, weeping silently to herself all the while.

We all felt desperate to do more than just look and talk. We wanted to scrub floors, light fires, chip the rotting paint from the walls, wash and dress the residents. But we had no brushes, no disinfectant, no mops, and only a motley selection of clothes to give out. So we had to stand back and content ourselves with writing endless lists of what we needed, identifying the most serious problems and trying to work out a plan of campaign to tackle them.

Top of the list came heating. The only fires working were in the staff room – which didn't count – the flooded basement room and in the pavilion, the two areas where we had found residents on our first visit. The temperature outside was approaching minus 10 degrees during the day and was much lower at night, while the beds in the draughty rooms were made with just a single thin, and usually damp, blanket. Most of the residents sensibly shared, with anything up to five in a bed for maximum body heat.

The problem lay in the *sorbas*, the solid fuel stoves made of clay and enamelled tiles that were to be found in almost every room. Apart from the three in use they were all broken, with tiles missing or their cast iron doors gone, chimneys with gaping holes or impossibly blocked with solid black sediment. My attempt to find someone to repair them resulted in my first arguments with those in authority at Podriga, and thus began the battles that were to become the hallmark of our stay.

It's okay, I was told, someone was coming to fix the *sorbas*.

'When?'

'Tomorrow morning.'

But the next morning no one ever came. I drove back to Saveni to find Marcan, the hospital administrator, who told me he would put someone on to it straight away. The following day there was still no one there to mend the stoves, and I stormed into Marcan's office telling him I would go and find someone myself even if it meant driving all the way to Buchecha to bring the man who mended Yonashen's *sorbas*.

'Oh no, you won't,' I was abruptly ordered. 'Podriga is part of Saveni Hospital and we employ our own *sorba* man. He's busy here at the moment but as soon as he has time he'll go up to Podriga.'

The same law was laid down to me regarding any tradespeople working at Podriga. Saveni Hospital had its own plumber, its own electrician, its own carpenter, and we were not allowed to seek outside help, despite the fact that the hospital employees were busy and we were prepared to pay for private contractors ourselves.

The Saveni *sorba* man, when he eventually arrived, had no supply of tiles, *sorba* doors or plaster with which to mend any of the stoves. We ended up driving to Yonashen to pinch all their reserves of these items, and at last the fires started burning once more. Fuel, though, was a problem. We tried to keep the stoves going almost constantly to keep both buildings warm, only to find the residents going round after us putting them out. The pathetic reserves of wood and coal dust behind the Pavilion were meant to last all winter and the residents did not believe our promise that we would find more from somewhere.

Relations with Marcan at Saveni Hospital seemed to be on a continuing downward spiral. Before our arrival the mayor had arranged for us to eat our evening meal up at the Saveni Hospital kitchens. On that first Monday we had just reached our hotel room feeling shattered and emotional after a long day up at Podriga, when Marcan and Alexandrovich knocked on the door demanding to know what we were up to and why we were late for the meal. They'd been waiting for us, they said. The other girls opted out and it was left to Andrew and me to walk up the hill to the hospital, although I wasn't feeling in the slightest bit hungry, and if I'd known what was coming I would have hidden down my bed and pretended to be asleep. We were both totally unprepared for the onslaught that came as soon as we'd stepped out of the hotel building.

'Why didn't you come to see us this morning? We were waiting for you to discuss the work we want your team to carry out. How dare you think you can just waltz up to Podriga and do what you like without our knowledge?'

I apologized profusely, trying to explain that we needed to gain a better picture of daily life at Podriga before we could make plans about how to help. There was no placating them, however.

'We've told you exactly what we need. All you need to do is come up with the goods.'

They then launched into an extraordinary attack on our friendliness with the mayor. They had evidently just learnt of the meal the mayor had laid on for us the previous evening, and for some reason they were furious about it.

'How dare you go to him for help? We are in charge at Podriga, the mayor has nothing to do with it – his jurisdiction doesn't go beyond the town boundaries and

Podriga is no concern of his. You come to *us* if you want accommodation and storage space, you come to *us* if you want food and contacts. Whom are you here to help – us or the Town Hall? You don't need to have any contact with the mayor or his cronies. Is that clear?'

The aggression and anger in their voices was frightening. What the hell was going on here? I began to realize that we must be caught up in some battle that was way over our heads, and we evidently had a great deal to learn of the local politics and rivalries of this strange backwater town.

Marcan moved on to the question of who was in charge of our group. Who was the boss? Who could he deal with? He seemed to think we had some director of aid operations down in Bucharest who gave us our orders, who provided us with funds. I procrastinated as much as I could, mumbling about people in Edinburgh and London.

'So with whom do I discuss serious proposals?'

My reply that, since I was the only one of us who could speak Romanian, it would have to be me, produced guffaws of laughter.

'A girl! Don't be so ridiculous! A girl can't deal with anything like drains or water supplies, plumbing or heating. How do you expect us to take you seriously? You're just a bunch of children, and if you're in charge of the pathetic set-up then we can't work with you.'

Only Andrew grabbing me stopped me from turning back and telling them to go to hell. I fumed in silence as we walked up round the back of the hospital, following them past empty sheds and stacks of coal. It was pitch dark and suddenly I froze, convinced that they'd brought us here to beat us up. They looked such thugs, and I couldn't stop thinking of the stories I'd heard about the couple who'd tried to work at Podriga in the spring who had somehow ended up badly hurt. I clutched on to Andrew and urged him to run back while we had the chance. Alexandrovich must have heard the panic in my voice, for he laughed and called out that we were almost at the kitchens now. I felt stupid and paranoid. I ordered myself to swallow my pride and my fears.

We sat down at a small table in a corridor. I took a deep breath and began grovelling. I apologized profusely for everything we'd done wrong, for not being a man, for having gone to the mayor for help. I explained that Andrew was definitely the boss – did I really forget to mention that before? – but they'd have to talk through me for the time being since there weren't any male translators available.

Sarcasm was fortunately lost on them and they became more amiable. We began discussing the water. I had already discovered that this was going to be the single biggest obstacle to achieving decent standards at Podriga, and no solution was going to be cheap. FARA had put us in touch with an engineer in Suchava whom they had paid to carry out a survey, and its results made depressing reading. The present situation was appalling. Podriga used two wells, one in the grounds providing just enough for the elementary washing machine in the basement, and the other in the village pumping up a trickle of water for about an hour a day through three taps, one in the kitchen, one in the downstairs toilet and one in the Pavilion. Both supplies had been tested by the Health Ministry the previous year with analyses of 'unfit for human consumption', and I had learnt from staff and residents at Podriga that both often dried completely in summer.

As I tried to discuss the options I realized I had to be careful – Marcan was trying to catch me out. They had decided on the water scheme they wanted – to sink a well further down the valley and pump it up into a storage tower – and whenever I suggested alternatives they sneered and laughed, obviously hoping that I'd agree so that they could say, 'Ha! We told you a girl could know nothing about water systems.' Since they were right, I did know absolutely nothing about water systems, this was hard work, but somehow I managed to fight them off with some desperate use of common sense. Never had a law degree seemed so utterly useless; again and again I longed to be a plumber or an electrician or an engineer.

In fact I tried to make the most of my legal training, rapidly inventing British charity law and, I thought, making it sound quite convincing. I informed them that we were not allowed to spend any donated moneys on a project unless we could present evidence to the Charity Commission that we had investigated at least three alternative viable options. I said that we would be bringing over our own specialists to look into Podriga's problems; we needed Marcan's advice, of course, but we were not able to simply give him the money – it was against the law.

Lies, lies, lies – the bullshit spouting from my mouth shocked even me, but somehow I had to stall for time without simply informing them that we didn't trust them an inch, and that we didn't have any money. Alexandrovich kept saying to me, with the smarmy smile always on his face: 'You don't really have any funds at all, do you? You're just wasting our time.' I thanked God for Yonashen, happily taking all the credit for what had happened there.

'Look what we've done at Yonashen,' I kept replying. 'How can you say that we won't see it through, that we're not committed?'

At one point Marcan turned to me and said: 'It'll be much harder changing things at Podriga than at Yonashen.'

I looked at him, and I thought, Yup, and the reason is sitting right in front of me.

Back at the hotel room Maureen poured me a huge vodka and I sat back on my bed wondering what we were doing. What arrogance I had had to assume that I was capable of changing anything here. I had never been more aware of my own lack of abilities and qualifications; this thing we were fighting was too big for me, and I was ready to give up.

The others, however, wouldn't let me, and I knew that what they were saying was true – it was either us doing our best, unqualified and unfunded as we were, or nothing for the Podriga residents. And anyway, they said, they had no intention of giving up yet, and they needed a translator.

Chapter 11

Siberian Setbacks

The bonds grew fast between our small group. None of us had known each other very well at Yonashen but, cooped up each evening in our two small hotel rooms, our characters were soon laid bare.

Colette assigned herself the role of cheerleader. Always chirpy, constantly singing, her beautiful Irish voice could be heard ringing through the cold Podriga walls from the moment we arrived in the morning. She looked like some latter day Davy Crocket, her head always clad in a huge rabbit fur hat with her bright little face smiling beneath it. I've never known anyone be so damn cheerful while unblocking loos or shovelling shit, and she never failed to perk me up when my spirits were flagging.

Maureen was more of an enigma. She was always sensible and level-headed. From the day we arrived her nursing abilities were put to full use as she dressed the appalling sores and scabies of so many of the Podriga residents, and the staff too were soon coming to her with their medical problems. More than the rest of us she came up against the hostility of Marishika and the medical assistants, for she was always being accused of 'disrupting the routine'. They pressured her to hand over her meagre supplies of dressings, antiseptics and painkillers, but she stood up to them resolutely and in the end commanded respect. In the evenings, though, Maureen transformed herself into the great joker. She would have us all in stitches as she described the setbacks of the day; she made fun of everyone, us and herself included, and thereby managed to take the heat from many of the disputes we found ourselves involved in.

Aileen's quiet surface hid a lively character, and a determination to succeed at Podriga that soon made her the central force of our small group. Her energy reserves were formidable; when the rest of us could hardly even crawl to our beds in the evening, she would set off through the snow to take the dogs for a walk. In the morning when I was struggling to open my eyes I would always hear her infectious laugh as she chattered over the tea-making; when the car wouldn't start in the morning and I was cursing and spitting, Aileen would merrily make the four mile walk to Podriga without so much as a complaint. At Podriga, her gentle manner had a wonderful effect on the residents, especially the most withdrawn and mistrustful of them. They would open up to Aileen when no one else could get near. Watching her working quietly in the dining room or Pavilion never failed to fill me with inspiration for what we were doing at Podriga.

Aileen also played the bagpipes, and she had them sent out to Saveni soon after our arrival. To watch someone so tiny produce enough blast to create the incredible sounds that came from those pipes was quite extraordinary – the rest of us could never manage more than very pathetic squeaks. Aileen would grow embarrassed when people watched her play so she would practise alone in one of the bedrooms, but the tunes would blast through half the town and sometimes crowds of Romanians would gather outside. Occasionally she took the pipes up to Podriga and played from one of the towers; it would silence residents and staff alike, and such occasions bring back my most haunting memories of the place.

Andrew's commitment to Podriga was total from the

beginning. While the rest of us were caught up in day to day concerns, Andrew made plans for the future, trying to devise solutions to the problems of fuel, of water, and where the money was coming from. During those first weeks he assigned himself the most tedious tasks: sitting in the telephone exchange in Saveni for hour after hour trying to secure funds from Britain; driving around searching for supplies; making list after list of what we needed. He found it frustrating that he had to leave all the dealings with Romanians to me, and he made a concerted effort to learn the language each evening – when I'd catch him reciting his verbs to the dogs.

At the end of November, Andrew flew to Edinburgh to secure proper funding. He tried to join one of the wealthier organizations dealing with Romania, but had no luck. The big league Romanian charities were confined to spending money on children's homes – we kept having it rammed down our throats that children had to come first, and there was apparently no cash left over for anyone else. The fact that the children would one day grow into adults was mysteriously forgotten. Only the Romanian Relief Fund promised to help, but their own cash supply was rapidly dwindling. Albania had just hit the headlines; the British public – quite justifiably considering the huge amounts that had been given overall since the revolution – felt that Romania had had its share of their generosity and had moved on to newer causes.

I visited the EC representative in Bucharest, a kind man up to his ears in demands who told me we stood little chance but we could submit a report of detailed and costed proposals for the next year's allocation of funds. He explained that the EC had got itself into a terrible mess by guaranteeing payment of all fuel supplies to children's institutions. The undertaking had been made soon after the revolution before anyone realized the scale of the problem. It was costing a fortune and he was now being ordered by Brussels to reduce the Romanian aid budget. I confided to him how out of our depth we felt; whereupon he told me that with a Romanian speaker, a vehicle, back-up from Yonashen and some small but loyal support groups at home, he thought we were much more likely to achieve some good than simply throwing EC money at the problem.

Back at Saveni, huddled with the others round our electric fan heater eating a bowl of revolting soya mince, it was difficult to share his optimism. After the first week we had cancelled the eating arrangement with Saveni Hospital – we were usually only given bread and jam anyway, and none of us could face discussions with Marcan and Alexandrovich after an exhausting day up at Podriga. We made do with a single electric ring in our room, eating supplies we had managed to pinch from Yonashen, together with what we could find from the shops in the town, which wasn't much. The bounty of the summer markets was long gone; we were lucky to find potatoes at the stalls and even eggs were a rarity. The contact system, whereby most townsfolk acquired their food from friends and relations in the country, we soon realized was not worth getting involved with. We were endlessly offered milk, meat and eggs, but at a price we could not afford to pay. They would not take money, instead demanding the clothes, medicines and cleaning stuffs that they knew we had – they had seen us unloading them into our hotel room.

We made frequent forays back to Yonashen to beg, steal and borrow what we could. Suddenly the orphanage seemed a house of luxury, while we were the poor relations. Moona took to running in the opposite direction whenever he saw me, yelling: 'Whatever it is, you can't have it!'.

Blondu began to realize that I wasn't gone for good and gradually the tears stopped. He'd greet me with soap and a towel pinched from the volunteers' room, knowing that I always wanted to head straight for the showers, and he often looked after the dogs for me when I was inside wheedling supplies from Jon and Moona. Emu was now working in *Triaj*, having taken over from Maureen, and seemed to be enjoying herself. I admired her enormously, knowing that it was a job I was incapable of. Blondu was not in her good books, however. She could not give him the same amount of attention as I had, and he was being difficult. I wished that I could take him to Podriga to explain to him what I was doing. I felt sure that it would help him understand, but I was terrified that once he knew where I was, he might then try and find his own way there.

We managed to find enough adult clothes in the Yonashen store to create an outfit for each resident, and at the end of the first week we held a dressing session in the room at the back of the Pavilion that had been assigned to us as a store. It proved to be total chaos. Not because of the residents, who quietly let us dress them and were delighted with even the mankiest of pullovers, but because some of the staff, whom we'd asked to help us, lost control entirely, grabbing armfuls of clothes and rushing off home with them. In an attempt to stop them stealing and to gain their support, we'd already given them a selection of the better stuff that we knew would only be ruined in Podriga's laundry, before writing 'Hospital Property' with an indelible marker pen on everything else. But this was no deterrent to some, and we wondered how long the residents would manage to keep what we had managed to get zipped and buttoned on to their pathetically thin bodies.

My old antagonist from Yonashen, the director Mitica, ironically proved to be one of our strongest allies in our fight to make changes at Podriga. Mitica's wife, Dana, worked for the Secretariat for the Handicapped in Botoshani. Bright, capable and fluent in English, she was thrilled that we were taking on what was apparently renowned as the most corruptly run institution in the region. She and Mitica offered to help us as much as they could, provided some good contacts and introductions for me in Botoshani, and Dana gave me some interesting information on what had been going on at Podriga over the past year. She had known Lee and Emma, the two aid workers who had been at Podriga. They hadn't stood a chance against Marcan, Headlice and their buddies, she said. At least six aid trucks that she knew of had unloaded vast quantities of clothes and equipment at Podriga – 'and you've seen how much of it is still there,' she said. She strongly suspected that Headlice was selling aid on the black market, and advised us to try and find evidence of this to get him sacked. Our best chance was to get him replaced by someone we could work with, as Moona had done at Yonashen, forcing the change from Doamna Jetta to Mitica.

Dana helped us compile reports to send to the Secretariat for the Handicapped in Bucharest requesting a transfer of authority from the Ministry of Health. This would take Podriga away from the control of Saveni Hospital. The prospect of not having to deal with Marcan and his cronies made me almost faint with longing. Again and again, though, we were turned down. I could hardly blame them for considering Podriga nothing but trouble and a bottomless pit of expenses, but at times I felt they were cutting off our only hope.

I spoke with the mayor about Marcan and Alexandrovich's verbal attack on our association with him; it transpired that the hospital management and the mayor's office were virtually at war. Up until the revolution Marcan had been number two Communist in Saveni, second only to the Communist mayor. The latter had lost his position, but Marcan had continued as administrator of the hospital since it was not a political post. The new mayor was young and defied the old Communist hardnuts. Marcan was jealous, and had no intention of giving up any of his power as, effectively, the employer of the largest workforce in town. The two men clearly loathed each other, both waiting to catch the other out, and we it seemed, had got caught up in the middle of their battle.

Slowly I learnt how to bargain with Marcan. Whenever I went to see him I'd hype myself up beforehand, pacing round the hotel room smoking far too many cigarettes as Colette drilled me:

'He needs us more than we need him. He won't get any brownie points for getting rid of us, and you're *not* scared of him, Sophie, you're *not*. Tell him if he doesn't send the plumber up today we're going to send an official complaint to Bucharest.'

Complaining to his immediate superiors in Botoshani had already proven futile, for we had visited them early on and it was clear that they didn't give a damn. But slowly small victories came. Marcan agreed to finance repairs to the roof (I found out later that he didn't in fact use any hospital funds, he got the money from the Ministry for Culture – Podriga was a listed historical building!) if we guaranteed to pay for the water. When I demanded to see the official fuel quota for Podriga, Marcan agreed to deliver some more wood the following week. I persuaded the hospital electrician to come up and fix the light switch in the basement room – up until then it had been turned on by twisting two live wires together just inches from the stream of brown liquid pouring down the walls – and he surveyed the building making a list of recommendations for me.

The arrival of our first aid delivery was a total disaster. It was due on a Saturday; on the Friday we drove over to Yonashen for more medical supplies and the Land Rover conked out. Guido was away and I forced Jon to work on it virtually at gun point but it was Sunday afternoon before it was going again. We raced over to Podriga to find the entire staff there: usually we were lucky to find a single care worker on a Sunday, as on our first visit when we'd found nobody except one of the cooks. Today, however, they were all there, full of smiles, welcoming us in, telling us what incredibly honest and Christian people they were. We found Gica, one of the fat sisters, standing guard over an impressive supply of clothes, disinfectants and cleaning equipment stacked up in the staff room. She instantly swept me up into her fulsome arms, told me that if it wasn't for her the whole lot would have been stolen, and what was I going to give her as her reward?

We never found out how much had disappeared before we arrived, but the simple move from the staff room over to our store in the Pavilion was enough of a farce. The staff, of course, all wanted to help, but we soon realized that the boxes of bleach and sacks of jumpers we were handing them were being taken nowhere near the Pavilion. We found them thrown under beds, in the attic, behind stoves, all ready for collection once we had gone. It was like a ludicrous game of hide and seek as we followed them round, and their lack of embarrassment upon being found out was breathtaking.

'But Colette told me to put it here,' said Anna as I caught her shoving a set of scrubbing brushes amongst the onions in the loft.

We stayed up almost all night writing inventories and marking clothes. Every few minutes one of us leapt up with shrieks of ecstasy upon discovering something that we particularly needed. When I saw the beautiful paint brushes that had been sent I decided I wanted to marry Edward Parry of the Romanian Relief Fund. At last we could get down to some serious work. We had fantastic thick sweatshirts to hand out to the residents the next day, mops to clean the loos with, disinfectants and bleach to do battle with the stench and the filth. It was a joyous evening and our hopes were high.

The next day the staff who'd somehow missed out on the previous day's fun pestered us continually with demands for their share.

'But Alexa's got a whole carton of bleach. She said you gave it to her.'

'I want one of those lovely red jumpers that Lenutsa's got.'

'I saw Karina wearing a beautiful jacket – have you any more the same?'

Meanwhile Aileen and Colette got stuck into the toilet areas, unblocking the drains and scrubbing the walls. The previous Friday we had managed to smuggle in a plumber from Saveni whom I'd met while scrounging for plastic piping around the building sites. He fixed a pipe into the ceiling of the downstairs toilet so that sewage no longer fell straight down on to our heads, but the pipe was too thin and the upstairs drain now kept blocking up. Scrubbing the walls we found nothing but layer after layer of grime. Colette decided that it would be more use scraping all the paint off, and for the next week she and Aileen looked like a pair of ghosts, perched up on ladders singing at the top of their voices as they hacked off 20 years' worth of caked-on filth and the white powder of the original paint.

Maureen spent her days quietly touring both buildings dressing sores, treating scabies and dispensing vitamin supplements and cups of fruit juice to the residents. Constantly she fought off a following of staff telling her of their sick children, mother, father, or husband. She would explain again and again that we didn't have enough supplies even for the residents: even so after a hard day at Podriga she was often to be found trudging through the village, visiting people with often chronic illnesses.

At the end of the third week we received a godsend. Colette, Aileen and I were scraping at the walls of the downstairs' toilet when one of the residents rushing in saying that some foreigners had just arrived. Hoping that it was the Yonashen Hilux van we rushed outside, but saw two cars with Dutch numberplates. A group of Western-looking people were walking towards us, accompanied by Marcan and Headlice looking very smug. They went past us without an acknowledgement and ignored our greetings as they entered the staff room. Incensed, I went in after them asking if anyone spoke English; Marcan promptly said that it was a private meeting. I ignored him, and after a painful silence was relieved to see an outstretched hand. An attractive blonde woman introduced herself as the representative of a Dutch charity called Dorkas. I explained that I was part of a team from the Romanian Project UK permanently stationed at Podriga, and she looked astonished.

'But I haven't been told anything about you,' she said and, as Marcan glowered at me, I explained our recent arrival. I learnt that some representatives from Dorkas had looked around Podriga just the day before our ominous first visit, and had been similarly appalled. They had returned to Holland and organized an articulated lorry load of beds, mattresses, clothes, and lighting and electrical equipment due to arrive the next day. I felt almost dizzy – the thought of replacing those filthy mattresses filled me with pure joy.

Nothing was ever simple at Podriga, however. The Dutch woman told us that the 'extremely helpful gentlemen' Mr Marcan and Mr Headlice were arranging the unloading and storage of all the aid, and that she and her colleagues would be leaving for Holland as soon as the trucks were empty. Alarm bells began ringing.

Knowing we had to act fast, as soon as we got the chance, we dragged her aside into the toilets, a place I knew Marcan wouldn't follow us. As she held her nose against the smell I tried to explain that if she handed over her supplies to Marcan and Headlice the chances of the residents ever seeing them were minimal. It was wonderful that they were bringing new beds and mattresses, but please would her team stay and oversee them actually being put into the bedrooms? Please would they unload their supplies into our store room so that they could be marked before being handed out to the residents? She looked rather shocked but said it sounded a reasonable plan and, almost choking by now, she returned to the staff room.

Apparently we had declared war. We sat outside the staff room listening in horror as Marcan, through a translator who seemed to be relishing the attack on us, informed the Dutch group that we were most definitely not to be trusted. Apparently all the aid that had arrived since we had been there we had stolen and sold on the black market. We never gave any of it to the residents, and we were just a supply base for Yonashen. (The latter charge we discovered was based on our having taken to Yonashen some children's clothes that had arrived amongst the supplies sent by the Romanian Relief Fund.) The police were supposedly worried about our activities and Marcan was hoping to have us removed from Podriga very soon. 'Look around you,' he said, innocent as pie. 'Can you see any good that they've done here?'

After all we had seen I couldn't believe we were now having to prove our integrity to a fellow aid group. But we succeeded and they decided to stay an extra day to see as much as they could actually handed over to the residents. When their truck finally arrived the following afternoon, almost the whole village turned up in the hope of ripe pickings. We suggested calling the police to get rid of them all, only to find that the Dutch were giving them presents of clothes in return for their 'help' with unloading. Pandemonium broke out as scores of people grabbed what they could and ran. They smashed the windows of our store room once they realized where the aid was being taken, and we watched helplessly as the 'delightful poor villagers' took the blankets and bedding that the residents so desperately needed. As we nailed planks across the gaping windows the Dutch group at last seemed to realize how naïve they had been, for that night they actually stayed at Podriga rather than return to their hotel in Botoshani. The beds and mattresses were not unpacked until last and it was too late to put them in the rooms, so we left them in the hall and the Dutch group slept on them, so terrified were they that they would all be gone by morning.

We persuaded them to bargain with Marcan the next day – they would take all the new beds back to Holland, they told him, unless they were allowed to burn all the stinking rotten mattresses currently in use.

Marcan was horrified. 'But they're government property,' he said. 'They're worth 3,000 *lei* each, you must pay for them if you burn them.'

Luckily the Dutch aid group ignored him and the bonfire we had that afternoon was an exhilarating sight. The joy of seeing all that stinking misery go up in flames was well worth the hole we must have been making in the ozone layer as thick black smoke rose up over the village. Every rusty, collapsing old iron bed was taken out and replaced by small, modern springy ones that the children bounced up and down on in delight for hours.

Dorkas had also brought a sizeable collection of furniture – chairs and tables that we dispersed around the rooms. The residents were thrilled, the staff horrified.

'But that's quality furniture, it must be worth a lot of money! They'll ruin it!' cried Marishika. 'Put it in the staff room, we need new tables and chairs. They can have our old stuff.'

'They don't need tables, it's not as if they can write or anything!'

'You can't carve "Podriga Hospital" into that chair! You're ruining it!'

Of particular attraction to the staff were two padded swivel chairs. I swear I could feel the hatred boring through my back as I wrote in indelible marker pen all over them. Marishika, in particular, had lost all her former charm.

'You're no different from us really! You sit in the staff room drinking coffee with us while the *bolnavi* wallow in their filth downstairs. You don't care about them any more than we do, you just don't want us to have anything!'

Despite the ructions with the staff, however, the aid from Holland gave us a huge boost in terms of what we could do for the residents. We put two blankets on almost all the beds and the bright mixed colours gave a sudden homeliness to the place after all the cold blue-grey of the regimental hospital bedding. Most of the clothing we had given out so far had already disappeared and we realized that our discreet markings in black pen were no disincentive at all to theft. While hating the lack of dignity it gave the residents we decided our priority had to be keeping them warm, so we set to work with a pot of red gloss paint on the clothes sent by the Dutch. Every item was soon marked on buttock or breast with a great red 'H'; some of the residents were understandably horrified, but most were simply overjoyed at the prospect of more layers.

One of the great disadvantages in being able to keep the residents warm, however, was the ensuing body lice population explosion. Lice like nothing more than layers of clean jumpers. They had been kept in check before by the cold and the residents' sparse coverings, but now, seemingly overnight, they were rampant in hair, clothes and bedding. We drove over to Yonashen and took their entire reserve of lice shampoo; we scoured the shops of Botoshani for insecticide, and then went to battle, but with the pathetic supply of water, lack of a single bathroom and the ever-plummeting outside temperatures, trying to wash all the residents at once was an almost impossible operation. We spent the morning changing sheets and covering the beds with insecticide, while frantically trying to keep the residents in the basement dining room and Pavilion day room. Cauldrons of all the available water were boiled on the kitchen stove before making a makeshift bathroom in one of the bedrooms. One by one the residents took off their clothes by the fire and stood in a small tub of soapy water as Maureen and I washed them with the shampoo. Then they had to dash through the freezing hall to another bedroom where Colette and Aileen wiped them down with scabies solution and dressed them in a clean set of clothes. Luckily the experience seemed not to be as degrading for them as we had feared. Most residents took huge delight in washing, and Maureen and I had great problems: first in stopping them all from stripping off and jumping into the tubs at once, then in persuading them to get out.

The other room was proving to be a haven for clothes' thieves. The entire sack of socks disappeared, causing me to be accused of 'cruel lying'. Socks were extremely precious to the residents; most still had no shoes (for some reason aid-donors always seem to forget about shoes – shoes and pants). Most were therefore understandably concerned about giving up their socks when we asked them to leave all their clothes behind in the first washing room.

'It's okay,' I told them. 'You'll be given some more, I promise.'

After the theft across the hall I kept finding them, clean and dressed but for their feet, scrabbling through the pile of lice-infested laundry in search of their socks.

'No, please! You're not allowed back in here, that's the whole point!'

'I'm never believing anything you tell me again. I want my socks!'

Slowly we grew to know the residents as individuals. Most were younger than their appearance suggested. Old Ioan, bedbound in one of the perishing rooms at the top of the main building, was only in his forties when I had presumed him to be a good seventy. He had had polio as a child and was unable to walk. His mother had cared for him until her death when Ioan was twenty-four, whereupon he had been sent to Podriga. He had been one of the first patients, and he told me of how it had been good in the beginning - clean, warm, and with far fewer residents. Year after year it had grown worse; they had simply been forgotten, he said. Ioan could read and he asked me for books. He lavished us with thanks whatever we brought him, and devoured any reading matter within hours. He grew particularly fond of William, my Dobermann. While Georgie and Smecky were chasing sticks outside, I would often find William upstairs sitting quietly beside Ioan's bed as the old man chatted to him.

Downstairs, one of the great characters was Ticutsa, a dark-haired woman in her mid-thirties who immediately adopted Maureen, or 'Mory' as she was called by residents and staff alike, as her best friend. Ticutsa managed to hold her own at Podriga much more successfully than most; she refused to have her head shaved, and she held on to most of her 'own' clothes by washing them herself and never letting them disappear down to the laundry in the basement. The staff left her alone mainly because she looked after the two children who lived in her room on the ground floor. Ticutsa saw Paulina and Marco as her personal responsibility; she fed them, washed them and clothed them, and consequently they had a much better life than the other four children over in the Pavilion. Paulina was chronically crippled by what looked like cerebral palsy, although the damage to the left hand side of her head suggested that her handicap could have been caused by a physical blow. Although apparently nineteen years old it was difficult to believe it; she weighed just five stone and gave the appearance of being about ten. Yonashen gave a small wheelchair for her, and Ticutsa would wheel her about outside the building; Paulina's little smile as the sunshine hit her face was an uplifting sight. Marco, on the other hand, got about fine on his own. He too looked about ten; a funny little chap, never any trouble, exuberant in the amount of hugs he gave us, but he never spoke or communicated. Ticutsa dressed him up in the best of the children's clothes we were sent – we let her choose what she wanted for him and Paulina – and he would run about the building in a world of his own.

Over in the Pavilion, I grew fond of Christy, a young man of twenty who had spent his childhood at Siret, the 'Anneka Rice' orphanage made famous by the BBC the previous year. It never failed to amaze me how Christy, and also Mitica, could have lived in such appalling surroundings and come through it as such a balanced, intelligent human being. Christy picked up our English very quickly and would have us in stitches as he mimicked our various accents. Like Mitica he appeared to suffer from cerebral palsy. He too could get around surprisingly speedily on his own, but he was much better than Mitica at persuading other more able-bodied residents to push him around in the wheelchairs we found for them.

As we grew fond of some residents, we also began to realize that others were the cause of terrible cruelty and violence. The prime culprit was a man of about forty named Doru. We began to notice how he was often wearing clothes that had just been given to somebody else, how he often appeared to be drunk, how the others always let him have his own way. Marishica came to us one day with appalling bruises saying that Doru had stolen the wood she had chopped and attacked her when she tried to stop him. We then found a great pile of clothes under his mattress and learnt that he was selling them to villagers for money, *tsuica* and cigarettes.

In early December we saw the true seriousness of the situation when a British physiotherapist, David, who had come over from Yonashen to help us, was dressing residents in the Pavilion. Aileen, Andrew and I were washing the children and saw Doru come into the room and take a whole pile of clothes. David told him to put them back, whereupon Doru pulled a knife from his trouser pocket and attacked him. The look on Doru's face was truly terrifying and if Andrew hadn't been there to pull him off I'm convinced Doru would have tried to kill him. It brought home to us that we were not dealing with kids here; there were some seriously disturbed men of great strength who were in positions of power at Podriga, which they had no intention of giving up just because we had arrived.

We spoke to the staff about having Doru removed to a more suitable establishment. Most seemed keen, for they too were terrified of him and rarely dared to cross him. Headlice though, was vehemently against the idea.

'Doru makes life more stable at Podriga,' I was told. 'If Doru goes, there will be a dozen other residents fighting for top position.' Headlice was using Doru to do his job for him – with Doru as undisputed king, the other residents were kept subdued and in their place. Headlice didn't give a damn about the selling of donated clothes, of course, and seemed to find the volunteers' fear of Doru amusing.

Eventually we did succeed in having Doru moved on, after calling on much higher authority within the Ministry of Health. He went to Botoshani Psychiatric Hospital Four, universally referred to as 'Psychy Number Four', a place which filled us with dread until we finally went there and found it to be far far better than Podriga. After Doru's departure Headlice's prophecy to a certain extent came true, for another particularly strong middle-aged man from the Pavilion named Vasile began terrorizing residents, staff and volunteers alike. But we persevered and he too was moved to Psychy Number Four. After this an atmosphere of wonderful calm descended and improvements in the general well-being of the other residents came rapidly.

We were regularly sent new patients *from* Psychy Number Four, however, and over the winter Podriga's numbers went up to a hundred and ten, while there were still only sixty-six beds. Podriga was the dumping ground, not only of the local orphanages but of the region's hospitals too, and seeing the effect on those who arrived as they realized they had reached the end of the line – 'the last stop before hell' as one put it – was always deeply disturbing. Many arrived looking very normal and lively, but as over the first few days their heads were shaved, their clothes were taken from them and often never seen again, they would often fall into a deep depression, taking to their beds and refusing to say a word. As we grew more used to Podriga's conditions this never failed to jolt us back to a realization of how truly awful the place was, and would fire our determination to somehow effect some changes.

Time flew by. Our days were full and frantic as we moved from one crisis to another, our understanding of Podriga and the system we were taking on slowly growing all the time. Our evenings were spent quietly in our hotel room; we were usually too exhausted to venture into the town bars and take on the endless interrogation that mixing with the townspeople entailed. So we stayed in, continually boiling up kettlefuls of water in a largely vain attempt to keep ourselves and our clothes clean. We were always filthy at the end of the day, smelling not unlike the Podriga toilets and often crawling with lice, resulting in our room being full of endless plastic bags full of clothes (a week away from the warmth and food of a body kills them). Our entertainment consisted of playing with the dogs, who were surprisingly good-humoured about having to spend their evenings in so confined a space. We usually took them up to Podriga with us during the day, where the residents would keep them amused for us – Georgie found a fifty-strong army of stick throwers.

Inadvertently we acquired a new puppy, which Colette found half-dead in the downstairs toilet at Podriga. She brought it back to Saveni with the intention of having it put to sleep, but when the time came we had all grown too fond of him. We tried to find him a home, but puppies are as overly plentiful in Romania as children and no one wanted a scruffy little runt who looked as though he wouldn't grow any bigger than a chihuahua. So Nipper stayed, amusing us for hours with his antics. He slept curled up inside my Russian hat and usually travelled in Collette's jacket pocket, looking out with envy at the other dogs as if dreaming of the time when he'd be as big as William.

I brought Hannibal over from Yonashen in the trailer and he soon became a favourite with the residents. Podriga, like Yonashen, had a horse of its own to fetch supplies from Saveni, and a horseman named Vasile to care for him and drive the cart. Vasile agreed to take on Hannibal too, so he spent the days tethered in the Podriga grounds, giving rides to the residents and munching through the overgrown wilderness that had once been smart lawns. His nights he spent in Vasile's barn. Vasile was a wily old fellow whom I grew very fond of; he was incredibly rude about the care workers, and often about us too when he thought we weren't doing all we should, but his home just a few yards from the back of the Podriga building was always open to us. I began to use it as a refuge when I needed a break in the middle of the day. Vasile's wife Silvia would present me with a plate of fried eggs and *mamaliga* as soon as I came in, and twenty minutes of sitting by their fire hearing all the local gossip or playing with their grandchildren would usually restore my sanity.

At the beginning of December my Land Rover had a serious engine blow. Yonashen lent us a tiny old van but its steering was lethal, its tyres bald and its electrical system defunct. After I nearly killed myself skidding off the road to Botoshani on my way to fetch Andrew from the station, we gave up using it except when absolutely necessary. As the snow deepened and the temperatures fell to minus 30, we were effectively marooned in Saveni. We walked the three miles to Podriga, catching a ride on a horse and cart if we were lucky.

I began spending more time in town, mainly from laziness but also in an attempt to find a solution to the water problem. The mayor proved extremely helpful as I explored our options, providing me with maps of the area and introducing me to engineers in Saveni who could give me advice. Everyone said the same thing about the solution put forward by Marcan – the sinking of a new well would be extremely expensive and there would be a multitude of problems with regard to the continual pumping of water two kilometres up to Podriga. But, most importantly, the proposed site would still not provide enough water in a hot summer – we'd have to dig five kilometres from the village to be assured of a constant supply. I learnt a great deal about soil structure and water systems – that for instance you can't just dig deeper and deeper until you find the amount of water you need, that you could lose the lot if you reach a permeable layer that drains it all away – but I grew increasingly depressed about the prospect of ever seeing a flushing loo at Podriga.

In the middle of December I had a brainwave. I decided to stop thinking in terms of the wells that Romanians rely on to provide water in country areas, and think about what I would do at home if I lived in a house without water. Droughts over the past few years in the Lake District had left many villages and farms, including the one where my parents live, short of water. They had all been forced to pay for a connection to the mains supply – there had been no talk of sinking new wells. Triumphantly I marched into the mayor's office.

'Why can't we just lay a pipe along the road from Saveni, connecting Podriga to the town's water system?'

'It would be fine by me,' he said, and sent out his deputy to find the director of GOSCOM, the state company in charge of the town's water and drainage systems. I was introduced to a charming if not overly intelligent man named Mihai, who also saw no reason why my scheme would not be possible. Saveni, he told me, was fed by a reservoir about 10 kilometres west of the town. There was enough water to feed a population four times the size of Saveni, so there was easily enough surplus for Podriga. I suddenly remembered something.

'So why is the water in the town turned off for five hours during the day and after ten o'clock at night?' I asked.

He looked at me in astonishment. 'Why on earth do you need water all day and all night?' he asked, and I realized that I was about to become involved with yet another part of the chronic ex-Communist system that was stopping this country from functioning properly.

My Christmas deadline was fast approaching. There was no way I could leave Romania now; we'd only just begun, and the problems seemed to be increasing rather than getting any better. Thus once again I decided to stay longer. This time I didn't even try to put a date on when I'd be able to leave for good. The rate things were going we'd be stuck out here for years. But I'd promised my mum I'd be home for Christmas and I booked myself on to a flight on 20 December, returning a week later. Instantly I felt guilty about leaving Andrew and Aileen alone at such a time. Maureen had already returned to Scotland to replenish her money supply and Colette had recently had to rush back to Belfast. We'd just moved out of the hotel into an apartment in a block on the main Saveni street; there were four rooms and even a flushing loo, but no heating and no beds, and I imagined coming back to find the two remaining volunteers frozen solid to the concrete floors. All the drains at Podriga were frozen and the toilets were stinking quagmires. Aileen came back at the end of each day resembling a sewage worker, having spent hours bucketing it away from the building. The health of the residents seemed to be declining; there was constant coughing and wheezing and the residents all looked deathly pale. I set off for the airport praying that no one would die over the next week.

And I had thought that the last time had been a culture shock. I went straight from the airport by Underground to Oxford Circus, and as I walked down Regent's Street I began to feel faint. The Christmas lights, the smart shops with their beautiful displays, the crowds of shoppers laden with presents – it was too much. England wasn't like this when I left, I kept thinking. Saveni and Podriga might as well have been on another planet. I arrived at the offices of the Romanian Relief Fund and collapsed into a chair, suddenly aware of my filthy sweatshirt and leggings, hoping that I didn't smell too bad. Edward Parry, the Relief Fund's co-ordinator, was frantically printing out last-minute Christmas appeals and I sat looking round his office, perversely calmed by the haunting photos of horrific Romanian conditions on the walls.

The Relief Fund agreed to loan us a car; I could pick it up in Bucharest when I flew back. I heaved a huge sigh of relief and rang my mother to tell her I was home.

'Is Emu with you?'

I'd been desperately hoping that Emu would already be back in England, but she obviously wasn't. We'd had no contact with Yonashen for ages; the phone lines had been down for over a week and for all I knew they were all completely snowed in. Shamefacedly I had to tell my mother that I had no idea where my sister was. I knew that she intended to be back for Christmas, and knowing Emu she would make it somehow, but Romania suddenly seemed a very long way away.

Emu did in fact make it back before the 25th, having driven with Mike in his faithful truck. She was heartbroken about having to leave the *Triaj* kids and could barely talk about them without crying. As we saw old friends I recognized her inability to relate Yonashen to anything at home.

'So what's it like? Is it really as awful as it looked on the telly? Were the kids sweet?'

'Um, yes, I suppose so . . . well, not really . . . I don't know . . .'

We had a quiet family Christmas, and then I rushed down to Manchester to talk to experts at North West Water, who explained how to carry out tests on Podriga's present supplies to see if they were really as bad as we'd been told. In London I met Colette who was arriving from Belfast. My grandmother had given me 200 pounds for Christmas so Colette and I went wild in the Christmas Sales, arriving at Stansted Airport the next day laden with four electric radiators, an oven, kettles, a typewriter and dozens of hot water bottles. We found the Relief Fund's Lada in Bucharest and made a terrifying ten-hour journey to Saveni through driving snow.

New Year was miserable. The four of us toasted it in with mugfuls of the Bailey's Irish Cream that Colette and I had bought at the airport, but next door in my room William lay dying. The day after I left he had been hit by a lorry on the road to Podriga while Andrew was hitching a ride in a cart. He had seemed all right at first, with no bones broken, but he hadn't eaten anything since Christmas and by the time I saw him he was little more than skin and bone. He was retching foul-smelling blood and could hardly hold his head up. I found a vet, who proudly announced that William had worms and gave him appropriate injections. I should have had him put to sleep but I kept hoping he'd get better; too late we realized that he had internal bleeding and probably a ruptured spleen. He died in my arms at three in the morning on the second of January, and I'm crying even writing about it now. William had saved my life the previous May; I hadn't been able to save his and I felt absolutely miserable.

William's death set the tone for January. The problems at Podriga got worse and worse. Sixteen new residents arrived. The staff instantly shaved their heads and they wandered round in deep shock. But worst of all, Fiona had come over from Yonashen and identified the cause of all the coughing. We had a TB epidemic on our hands.

It was terrifying. Saveni Hospital refused to admit people doubled up and moaning in pain, and we had no way of keeping them warm and dry or isolated from the other residents. Marika, a young gypsy girl who slept in one of the freezing rooms upstairs, went downhill very fast and we feared for her life. We ended up practically kidnapping the worst cases. Andrew and Silvia, one of the better care workers who had suffered herself from TB, bundled them into the Lada and took them on an hour and a half journey to a TB centre we'd been told about. We found an impressively well-run place with a friendly director who agreed to admit them, and over the next few weeks we made many return journeys as more and more residents went down with the disease.

Our sanitary nightmare continued as the drains continued to freeze solid. I hired GOSCOM, the Saveni water and drainage firm, to come and unblock them, but they said they could do nothing until the weather improved. Almost all the Dutch bedding and most of the jumpers had disappeared and we were reaching a crisis point as to how to keep the residents warm. Firewood was nowhere to be found, no matter how much we were prepared to pay for it, and I had to get down on my knees and beg Marcan for more of the hospital's plentiful supplies. Residents scrabbled about in the rubbish tip for anything to burn. For the time being we'd given up trying to wash them – the risk of pneumonia was too great – and along with them we went through the whole of January without a bath or a shower. I caught a bad dose of worms that drained me of all energy and drive and resulted in a terrible cough that for a while convinced me that I'd caught TB.

In January we also made a frightening discovery about a practice that the Podriga staff had so far successfully hidden from us – drug abuse. While refusing to send antiseptic solutions or bandages up to Podriga, we learnt that Saveni Hospital gave the staff vast supplies of phenobarbitol and tranquillizer tablets. They were administered randomly by the untrained care workers whenever they wanted to shut someone up, with no record of amounts given or to whom. Some of the residents, including the children in the Pavilion, were daily receiving potentially lethal cocktails of unmarked pills that the staff kept in coffee jars in their pockets.

Meanwhile we were informed by friends in Saveni that we were under surveillance by the Securitate – the secret police – and more than once we were convinced that our apartment had been searched. Suddenly the police in Botoshani began refusing to renew our visas, and our application for a phone line was turned down again and again because Saveni Hospital refused to sign the piece of paper confirming that we needed a phone for aid purposes. It seemed a concerted effort was being made to get rid of us. Snowed in and without any easy way to communicate with the outside world, it was hard not to feel frightened – if we all disappeared no one would know about it for weeks.

I wondered if things could possibly get any worse.

The turning point came suddenly. An aid truck sent by the Wandsworth Charity Trust managed to fight through the snow and reached us by the end of January. Never had a lorry looked more beautiful as it skidded its way up the drive. Prisoners and officers from Wandsworth Prison had sent us crate upon crate of superbly indestructible prison uniforms and bedding, thick warm boots, high concentrate bleach and disinfectants. It quite literally saved our skins. With it came Maureen and Robert, a carpenter who had worked at Yonashen and now joined our team, setting to work on the broken windows and doors.

My mother sent out a chest full of electrical equipment in the truck, and a week later two electricians from her firm arrived at Suchava Station. Pete and Rob were here for a month to completely rewire both buildings and they set to work immediately in the Pavilion, fascinating the residents as they began drilling through the walls and laying the conduit. Pete accompanied me to the electricity board in Botoshani and we organized new incoming cables from the main power line in the village – the present supply wasn't even enough for all lights to be switched on at once. We bought a television and soon the Pavilion became the place to be at Podriga for both residents and staff as they crowded round to watch the fuzzy black and white picture. The new sockets also meant that we could plug in radios and tape recorders. They injected life and laughter into the cold grey rooms, and residents who previously hadn't said a word to us were suddenly making requests for their favourite music to be played. We began holding dances in the evenings. I don't know who enjoyed them more, us or the residents, as we alternated between British pop, Irish folk and traditional Romanian music. The staff would look on in amazement, shaking their heads at our madness.

In February the weather rapidly improved and finally GOSCOM came to unblock the drains. Ten men arrived with a bowser and blasted out a whole tankerload of accumulated filth but said they couldn't do anything to ensure a constant flow – without water to flush through the system, there were simply too many solids. Marcan was furious when he found out about GOSCOM's involvement. If we were going to pay people to unblock the drains, he said, then we should have paid him and he would have sent men up from the hospital to do the work. I reminded him that I'd been pestering him for two months about it and he'd done absolutely nothing.

'I didn't know you were offering money,' he replied.

Gradually we built up our numbers, hoping that our presence was by now well enough established to withstand Saveni Hospital's disapproval. Collette Pollard, our old ally from Yonashen, came out in February, and brought her brother Paddy with her. Paddy's mohawk haircut was a constant source of wonder to the Romanians, but he quickly grew very popular and he ended up staying at Podriga longer than any of us. At last more time could be spent on the actual care of the residents. Aileen spent hours down in the basement encouraging reading and writing, drawing and singing, while Collette sat in the ladies' rooms helping them with knitting and embroidery. Rob, one of the electricians, decided like so many of us before him that he didn't want to go back to England yet. He ended up staying for six months and was one of the most dedicated volunteers I've known, spending his free time enticing the residents up from the basement to play football outside, always laughing, smiling, optimistic. The apartment became a noisy den of chaos as we squeezed into the five beds and tried to concoct meals for ten out of a tin of corned beef or a packet of soup.

In February I also had a visit from my father. He was in Romania representing the Parliamentary Human Rights' Committee investigating abuses in psychiatric institutions, and I saw a chance to force the Bucharest authorities into awareness of what was happening at Podriga. My father came up trumps. He brought a journalist and a photographer from *The Times* to spend a day with us, and then I accompanied him to meetings in Bucharest with the Health Minister.

The latter proved to be a fool – when I asked him how many hospitals under his authority had no water, no doctor and no heating, he replied: 'But I do not always have water or heating in my own home, and I do not always have a doctor on call!'

None of the officials were prepared to admit to outside observers that their problems were anything but financial. Mismanagement was repeatedly denied, and I thought I was going to be forcibly evicted from the meeting as I kept popping up saying, 'But at Podriga . . .'

It paid off, however. Ten days later, with a full page article about Podriga in *The Times* which brought in a welcome injection of cash and an ensuing programme about us broadcast across Europe on the 'Europa Libera' radio station, the Health Ministry sent up a representative to investigate our allegations. Marcan and Headlice were given a stern ticking off and ordered to stop being so antagonistic, and suddenly we were given our phone line and our visas. But the most important result was the decision that Podriga should have a full-time doctor to run it. Our spirits soared – if we could find someone good, our problems with the staff and the Saveni management were over.

February's other highlight was the visit of 'the water boys' – Pete, an engineer from Southern Water, and Ron, a building contractor from Woking. I spent a week desperately trying to translate technical terms whose meaning I didn't even understand in English, as they hammered out details of a workable way to connect Podriga to the Saveni water mains. It was an exciting time as we realized that it was really going to happen. An engineer from the Prefect's office in Botoshani came out to give the legal go-ahead and agreed that the Town Hall would pay for a detailed topographical survey of the proposed route. We had to find the materials in Britain, and Ron's firm would come out to do the work in the summer (the pipes couldn't be laid until the ground had thawed). GOSCOM would make the connection to the water purification plant on the hill above the town and hopefully by the end of August, Podriga would have twenty-four hour running water. We planned to put five public stand pipes in the village to alleviate the general water shortage, which we hoped would also ensure the maintenance of the system once we had gone.

Andrew returned to Edinburgh once more to raise the 12,000 pounds needed for the pipes. Everything was suddenly coming together. The weather was rapidly getting warmer, with a corresponding improvement in both our and the residents' health, and everyone was smiling a lot more. Now that the paint no longer froze on contact with the walls we began redecorating the rooms, buying posters and paintings to cover the areas of mould and damp. A surveyor came out from Ireland to advise us on what we should do about the long-term requirements of the buildings. His report made depressing reading – the place was falling to pieces – but at least we now had plans for improvement.

Chapter 12

Blondu Disappears

At the beginning of March something happened that took my mind completely away from Podriga affairs. I rang through to Yonashen one afternoon wanting to talk to Moona, and Lenutsa, my old friend-cum-foe from the kitchen staff, picked up the phone. I began to ask how she was, but as soon as she'd established my identity she began yelling at me. The fuzzy line and her shrieking voice made it difficult to understand what she was saying; she always used to call me Blondie and I thought she was just hailing a greeting. At last I worked it out.

'Have you got Blondu with you?' she was asking.

'No, of course not.'

'He ran away on Saturday and we thought he was with you, we've been trying to contact you,' she said.

It was now Wednesday – Blondu had been missing for five days. I spoke to Jon who said that he'd disappeared whilst on a walk in the forest with Diane. They'd been searching through the woods but had pretty much given up – no one had a clue where he could have got to.

I tried to busy myself with a report I was writing back at the apartment but I found I couldn't stop shaking. I kept thinking of how vulnerable he was, a deaf child with no means of telling people where he came from if he wanted to go home. Though the weather was warmer now it was still below freezing at night. He didn't have any money on him and, despite his excellent pick-pocketing abilities, he'd be starving by now. Jon said they were all sure that he'd been taken in by some family and was probably being well-looked after, but I found that impossible to believe. For a couple of days, yes, but no one would keep him longer without informing the authorities or kicking him out. Romanians simply didn't take in outsiders like that, especially handicapped ones – if they did there wouldn't be all those kids stuck in Yonashen in the first place.

When the others came back from Podriga I found myself bursting into tears as I told them the news. They agreed that I should take the car and have a search for him. Most of Blondu's knowledge of the area outside Yonashen's immediate surroundings had been learnt on his car journeys with me the previous summer, and I felt sure that he would head for places familiar. So I drove into Botoshani and revisited our old haunts, scanning the market and the main street. Within an hour I'd had a sighting, at one of the restaurants I'd sometimes taken him to. As soon as I entered a waitress approached me.

'Are you looking for that little boy you used to come here with last year? He was here about three hours ago.'

'Are you sure?'

'He was the blond, deaf one with the big ears – the one we all liked. I recognized him, that was why I didn't chase him out like we usually do with the street kids. He sat down at that table in the corner and I brought him a bowl of soup. He didn't have any money but he gave me a flower. He was wearing rubber boots and a green coat, although he looked very dirty.'

To her astonishment I kissed her, and I ran out cursing myself – if I'd come to look as soon as I'd made that phone call I would probably have caught him in there. I knew he must be near and I scanned the vicinity. I'm surprised I wasn't arrested for child molesting – I kept rushing up and grabbing children of the right height, convinced it

must be him. The task was made a hundred times harder
by the woolly hats that all Romanian children wear when
outdoors, so I couldn't just look for the familiar white head
with big ears.

The manageress of a cafe in the square a few hundred
yards away claimed she'd seen him the day before, playing
outside with gypsy kids. She'd especially noticed him, she
said, because it was so unusual to see a blond child among
the mob of gypsy youngsters always hanging around the
centre of town. She'd gone up to him and asked him where
his mother was, but he'd seemed to be a simpleton, she
shrugged, for he'd just grinned at her and run off.

This was quite good news. If Blondu was living amongst
the gypsies he was probably being fed and fairly well
looked after; he was competent enough at petty theft to
pay his way with them, and his natural friendliness would
probably endear him to them. There was a sizeable gypsy
population in Botoshani but I didn't know where to start
looking. It was also now dark and I was aware that I was
being stupid searching down unlit alleys on my own. I went
to see Dino, the journalist who'd worked at Yonashen the
year before and who had become a friend during my time
there, and he agreed to help. We went to the police, to the
hospital, to every orphanage and institution in the vicinity,
before walking down endless backstreets asking groups of
children if they'd seen a little deaf child with very blond
hair. We searched all the bars and the hotels. We woke up
children sleeping rough in doorways and shop entrances,
and I saw something of the Romanian urban underclass
which haunted me for weeks as I thought of how hard it
could be to find Blondu if he became a part of it. We asked
at the train station and the bus depot. Somehow Blondu
had reached Botoshani from Yonashen, and if it had been
by bus or train from Buchecha I thought he would probably
try to return by the same method. Unable to read or ask for
his destination he could be on his way to the other end of

the country. I prayed that he was on foot – if he reached Bucharest or one of the larger cities he'd be lost for ever. There were reckoned to be over 30,000 street children in Bucharest, runaways from orphanages and youngsters kicked out of their homes at terrifyingly young ages.

Finally we gave up and I drove to Yonashen to tell them what I'd learnt. I stayed the night and the next day was accompanied by Moona and Diana as I searched the market, the shops and the backstreets once more. Dino persuaded the local paper to print an announcement with Blondu's picture, but we concentrated on the gypsy community, sure that if he was somewhere in the town they would be far more likely to know about it than the police. We had no more sightings, however. He seemed to have vanished completely, and after still no luck the next day I grew convinced that he'd moved on from Botoshani.

I drove to Suchava, the other town that Blondu knew well, and spent the weekend with Victoria Hornby, the British girl running operations at Costina, a 'psychiatric hospital' much like Podriga on the other side of the Suchava River. Newspaper sellers in the square were sure they had seen Blondu on Friday afternoon – they described his clothing correctly and said he was filthy. Victoria knew someone at the local radio station and we had announcements of Blondu's details broadcast every hour. We wrote out a poster with his description and a photograph, made a hundred copies of it and begged every shopkeeper in the town to display it in their windows.

Back in Botoshani, Dino had strange news. After the newspaper announcement which had given Dino's home telephone number as a contact, he had received a call from someone claiming to have Blondu with him, demanding a 100,000 *lei* ransom. He arranged a time and a place to meet and went there with a plain clothes policeman but the man did not surface, nor did he contact Dino again. Dino convinced me that it was sure to be a hoax but the thought that there were people who would consider kidnapping a child in the hope of getting money out of the foreign aid workers in their midst worried me. I could not stop myself thinking of all the perverts out there; Blondu was so friendly and trusting, he would follow anyone who showed him kindness. The thought of someone hurting him made me feel physically ill. I felt I was going crazy. I couldn't drive anywhere without permanently scanning the roadsides, and my heart kept jumping to my mouth as I thought I saw him, only to drop once more when I realized I hadn't. I kept thinking how I was going to kill him when I found him, while wishing for it more than anything in the world.

Ten days after his disappearance there was still no sign of him. We'd had no more sightings since those first ones in the Botoshani restaurant and square and by the Suchava newspaper sellers, and I was sure that by now he must be out of the region. With all the posters, searchings and announcements, we would have heard something if he was staying with a family or running wild in the town. I decided we'd have to make the search a national one and made plans to contact newspapers in Bucharest.

Mitica, director of Yonashen, would have none of it. While insisting that Blondu was bound to be holed up in some peasant's house within a few miles of Yonashen, Mitica had banned volunteers from taking any child out of the orphanage gates and was desperately trying to find a scapegoat for the incident. Poor Diane was made to feel terrible; the fact that Blondu could have run away at any time by simply walking out of the back gate was irrelevant to Mitica. When I pointed this out he said he at least then would have been able to sack whichever gateman had been on duty, and he would have been seen by his superiors to have done something.

'But I can hardly sack Diane, can I?' he asked, as if expecting me to feel sorry for him.

Mitica's priority was under no circumstances to let his

superiors in Bucharest know what had happened. He might lose his job.

'They'll want to know why I didn't inform them straightaway, why I'd let a large group of children go walking in the forest with a single volunteer, and they'll judge me incompetent. Is that what you want, for me to be blamed for the trouble you volunteers cause? And anyway, there's no need for them to know – Blondu's bound to be somewhere close. He'll turn up soon.'

Mitica was angry enough that his immediate superior and close personal friend, the local chief of the Secretariat for the Handicapped, should have been told about it. I had always liked Mr Gushu before, but now, seeing his true colours, I was appalled. He reprimanded Mitica for not having been told earlier, while being vehement about not letting the Ministry in Bucharest know.

'It will reflect very badly on us,' he said. 'If you get me into trouble I swear I'll make life impossible for you lot at Yonashen, and I certainly won't do any more to help you transfer Podriga from the Health Authority.'

Appeals to his conscience achieved absolutely nothing, and as I badgered him daily to let me go down to Bucharest he grew more and more nasty. At one stage he lost his temper and let slip some appalling truths.

'But surely you'll have to report sooner or later that Blondu is missing, and it can only reflect well on you if you're seen to have done all you can to find him?' I asked.

He replied that he would not have to let Bucharest know – Blondu had no papers, no files, not even a name, so as far as officialdom was concerned he had never existed in the first place.

It transpired that before my time at Yonashen another child, quite seriously handicapped, had disappeared. No efforts had been made to look for him and he'd never been seen again. No one had ever informed Bucharest and no one had been in any trouble. Obviously they hoped that this disappearance would pass just as quietly, and I was disturbing their trouble-free world. Gushu became abusive, all his resentment of foreigners coming to a very strange and perverted head.

'How come you're so interested in this child, anyway?' he said to me. 'I've heard about you, that you have an abnormal interest in him. How do I know that something fishy isn't going on? I've heard stories of how you Westerners smuggle children out of the country, how you sell them for adoptions, and I think this is all a big scam. I don't believe that Blondu simply disappeared in the forest – it's too much of a coincidence that only a volunteer was there to see it. I think that you've taken him away somewhere, that all this concern of yours is just a cover-up so that we take the blame for it!'

I was too flabbergasted by this outburst to do anything more than bite my lip to try to stop my tears. A child's life was at stake and all these swine could think about was covering their own backs. And as usual I had to swallow the words that would have come out naturally, and try to be reasonable and not tell them what I thought of them, since I knew it could cause terrible harm to our future at Podriga and Yonashen if I antagonized them any more than I had to.

Most of the volunteers at Yonashen seemed to think I was over-reacting too.

'Stop worrying, he'll turn up any day with that great grin of his, right as rain,' said Jon.

'He's bound to be somewhere local,' insisted Mitica. 'And anyway, he's a tough kid, a survivor.'

At the back of my mind was also the possibility that he might be having a great time – Yonashen was a rotten place for a child to grow up in, so what was I doing trying to bring him back? But it was the only home he knew. I remembered his joy at coming back after his hospital stay and I was convinced that he wouldn't stay away this long voluntarily. I kept having nightmares, seeing him cold and frightened, desperate to get home but with no way of telling anyone who he was or where he came from. I cursed myself for not having foreseen this happening – I should have made sure he wore an ID bracelet, or taught him how to write Yonashen. I imagined him run over on busy roads, flattened by trains – being deaf he was so vulnerable out on his own.

Aware that I was neglecting my work at Podriga, that a too-close emotional bond with one child was stopping me from helping others, I also knew I'd never be at peace until I found him. As two weeks turned into three I decided to announce Blondu's appearance nationally whether Mitica and Gushu liked it or not, whether or not it caused trouble in our other work. Nothing at all was going to happen unless I forced it to. They were hoping that I would just give up and eventually forget about it, and I simply wasn't going to let that happen. I told them I was going down to Bucharest with or without their authority, and warned them that if they tried to stop me I'd kick up such a stink that they would definitely lose their jobs.

It worked. At last they gave me the go-ahead. They would allow it, they said, on the condition that I didn't mention Yonashen or the fact that Blondu was an orphan. Mitica gave me a piece of paper with the information I was to give out. On no account was I to tell people anything else, he ordered, and when I read it I laughed. It made Blondu sound like an umbrella that had been lost on the train. In fact Dino said it was a good idea not to mention that Blondu was an orphanage child, for if people thought they had seen him they would be much more likely to ring the contact number if they thought there were worried parents desperately waiting for word of him.

I caught the train down to Bucharest and headed straight for the television centre. I feared they'd probably show me the door but it was worth a try – a television announcement would have a hundred times more impact than a brief paragraph in a newspaper. Thanks to my being a Westerner I was taken straight up to the programme controller's office, where I found a kind old man who welcomed me in and asked what he could do for me. As I explained my mission he listened intently. He was moved, he said, that a foreign aid worker could care so much about a Romanian child, and he promised to help me. I ended up telling him the whole story of Blondu's disappearance and he brought me a cup of coffee and even some chocolate when I started crying. I watched as he arranged for an announcement to be made before the seven and nine o'clock news broadcasts. He agreed to give only the details on Mitica's piece of paper – it was all he needed, he said, and of course he didn't want me to be in trouble with the orphanage director. I gave him Blondu's photo and Dino's telephone number, and thanked him for restoring my faith in Romanians. I left feeling hopeful, praying that Blondu would soon be found, and aware that if this didn't provide any leads the options were running out.

Maureen and I proceeded to get very drunk as we waited at the airport for Aileen, flying back from a two-week break at home. The flight was delayed so we missed both sets of news. I was too frightened of calling Dino in case I blocked the telephone lines, so I decided to wait until we'd got back to Saveni the next day before seeing if there was any news.

On Sunday, however, I got no answer from Dino or Mitica. Both were out all day, and the Yonashen telephone rang unanswered in Mitica's locked office. I sat in the apartment waiting for news, cursing them all for not telling me what was going on. At last, on Monday morning, Dana, Mitica's wife, rang.

'He's home! We've just got back, we drove all night . . .'

The shrieks of joy from the apartment when I gave a thumbs-up sign to the others drowned any further communication for a while, but eventually I learnt more of the story. Five minutes after the first announcement, Dino was rung by a care worker from a psychiatric institution near Mogoshu, a town about 300 miles away in the middle of the Carpathian Mountains. She was sure it was the same child, she said, as a boy sent into their care ten days previously by the police, who had found him sleeping at the railway station. A detailed description convinced Dino that it really was Blondu and he had rung Mitica with the news. The three of them had set off for the place immediately. There was still snow in the mountains, Dana said, and the journey had taken eight hours. They had arrived on Sunday morning and found Blondu drugged and very dopey but extremely pleased to see them. Apparently he had burst into tears and clung on to them – he most definitely wanted to go home.

Once again he had arrived at Yonashen the returning hero, rushing round hugging and kissing everyone. Apparently he'd had some money in his pockets which he'd handed out to the other kids – he sounded pretty much his old self. Dana said he had lost weight but otherwise looked okay – he'd even had a haircut. The drugs they had given him had worn off – she wasn't sure what they were – and he was as lively and vivacious as ever.

Unable to contain myself I was soon driving over to Yonashen, desperate to see him in the flesh. It was difficult to believe that the nightmare was really over, that none of the terrible fates I'd been imagining had actually happened. When I finally saw him and swung him up into a hug, he seemed amazed to see me and acted as if I didn't know he'd even been away, and frantically trying to tell me of the exciting things that had been happening. Most of it I couldn't understand but there were a lot of trains in the story, and quite a bit of running. When I explained to him how worried I'd been, that I'd been crying and frightened, he had the grace to look shamefaced for a total of two seconds before launching back into his incomprehensible story. I so wished that he could talk and tell us exactly what had happened to him before he was sent into care by the police in Mogoshu. (In fact some of the details came out a few days later, when a woman from Suchava somewhat belatedly noticed one of my notices in a shop window. She rang to say she'd seen the child in the picture being put on a train by a policeman at the station in Vereshti, a village near Suchava, on a Friday evening two weeks ago. Enquiries revealed that the policeman had found him sleeping there; it was the end of his shift, and a Friday evening. He couldn't be bothered to take the boy into the station, with the endless hassles that would entail with filing reports, so instead he put him on a train heading for Timishoara, 800 miles away. Blondu had either decided to alight or been thrown off for lack of a ticket at Cresta, from where he must have caught another train to Mogoshu in the mountains.)

Anyway, he was home now and seemed to be fine, so I heaved a sigh of relief that at last I could get on with my life again. I was selfishly peeved that nobody at Yonashen even bothered to say well done or thank you. The Romanian staff all informed me that the director had found him – wasn't he clever? – and when Jon came up to me saying, 'You see, I told you he'd be fine, didn't I?' I nearly hit him. Mainly I just wanted a pat on the back for what had been a hard fight, but I also wanted some kind of acknowledgement that it had taken such efforts to find him and that it had not just been a simple matter of time. I was very aware that if I hadn't happened to have such a close bond with Blondu, he would probably have stayed at that psychiatric institution in Mogoshu for good – that if it had been another child, it would have been the end of him as far as Yonashen was concerned, like the child who had disappeared before.

I drove back towards Saveni and decided to stop in

Botoshani to see Dino and thank him for all his help. He frantically waved to me as he saw me getting out of the car and began yelling out of his apartment window.

'Have you heard about Blondu?'

'Yes!' I shouted back. 'I've just seen him!'

'No, that's not it. Something wonderful has happened – quick, come upstairs.'

I had no idea what he was talking about and as I entered the apartment I told him to slow down, unable to understand a word he was saying. He sat me down and said there had been another telephone call after the first one – his mother answered it because he had already left with Mitica and Dana for Mogoshu. A woman had rung sounding very timid and scared, saying that she had just been inundated with calls from friends and relatives who had been watching the television that evening. They had all told her that they recognized the child in the announcement, and could it really be her little Joseph, whom she had lost when he was just seven years old? He was deaf and dumb, she said, and had blue eyes and very blond hair. He had disappeared in 1986 and she had done all she could to find him but had eventually given up. Could it really be him?

I found myself hugging Dino with tears in my eyes. This was like a fairy tale, I could hardly believe it. Apparently the woman was coming over to Yonashen later in the week to see if Blondu really was her son. She hadn't said anything about wanting to take him home and I tried not to raise my hopes too high – after all, it might all be a mistake – but the possibility of him having a family who cared about him was so wonderful I felt like flying with happiness. Even if they couldn't manage him at home, just for him to have contact with them would be fantastic. It was brilliant, unbelievable news, and I immediately began wondering what they were like. The woman had not said where she lived, but I imagined a little village in the mountains such as the ones I had travelled through, where Blondu could fit into country life, looking after the animals and riding the horses.

It was by now the beginning of April and I had to get back to England quickly. The general election was being held on the 9th of April and, with my family's typical sense of dramatic timing, my elder sister was getting married two days later. There would be big trouble if I missed the latter event, having promised Jo months ago to go, and I needed to be at the former. If all the polls being broadcast by the World Service were right, my father was about to be another unemployment figure and I wanted to be there to help with the disappointment. Blondu had been found just in time. I had been delaying my departure until he was safe, and even had a nightmare about arriving at the church still dressed in my tatty old Podriga garb, crawling with lice and smelling of sewage, having just stepped off the plane on the 11th.

In fact I drove back with Evie, reliving our journey of the previous August. I was back in time for the last four days of the election and the frantic work of campaigning proved to be the best way to have a complete break from Romania. I hardly had a minute to think about Podriga, although in fact the chaos and the exhaustion, the refusal to let oneself consider failure, were remarkably similar to the work I was used to. After three recounts my father squeezed in by 185 votes, and the celebrating continued until my sister was good and married on the Saturday.

Shortly afterwards I saw Fiona, who had just come back from Yonashen and was starting work at St Thomas's Hospital in London, and she told me about the visit of Blondu's mother. She was quite an old lady with four other children, one of whom was also deaf. Blondu had recognized her instantly and leapt into her arms. There was no mistaking that she really was his mother, and everyone had been very moved. Apparently he had simply wandered off one day without a trace. In those days, at the height of Ceauşescu's severest years, you were not allowed to advertise for a child in newspapers or the television, nor even able to put up notices in the street. The police had done nothing but take down the details and file them away, and month after month his family had heard nothing until they had convinced themselves that he must be dead.

So much for all my dreams of an idyllic mountain village. Blondu came from the centre of Yash, the capital city of Moldavia, and his family lived in an apartment block. But his mother wanted him home and a week after her visit Mitica and Dana had driven Blondu the 200 miles which six years previously he had somehow covered on his own. Mitica organized for national television to record the happy reunion, no doubt desperately hoping that this time his bosses would take note and give him some brownie points for being such a caring orphanage director. Diane went too and worried that the family seemed very poor, but Blondu had been adamant that he wanted to stay there. All we could do now was pray that it worked out – throwing money at them at this stage would cause much more harm than good.

Nevertheless it was wonderful news, just knowing that Blondu was with people who loved him and would always look out for him. He wouldn't end up somewhere like Podriga when he turned eighteen – he'd have a home and a family, and with his sense of survival he was bound to find a slot somewhere in society where he could get by well enough. Life would never be easy for him, but then it wasn't for anyone in Romania and at least he now had a chance to give it his best shot. I felt unbelievably happy and relieved, as if the responsibility had now been taken out of my hands. He was with someone who loved him more than I did, and knowing that made it much easier to accept that I couldn't do more for him.

Chapter 13

Tearing Myself Away

Over the next couple of weeks, as I enjoyed England like never before, I had time at last to sit back and think about what I was doing with my life. At the end of it I came to a decision that was the hardest I had made since I had set foot in that damned country that had come to mean everything to me.

My twenty-fifth birthday affected me deeply somehow, making me realize that the years were slipping by – I had been twenty-three when I first went to Romania. I vaguely remembered that I used to have plans and dreams for the life I wanted for myself, that once upon a time I'd been set on a career that I loved. My bank account was empty – I'd spent every penny I had on Podriga and the money from my book was long gone. For months now I'd been living off hand-outs from family and friends. It didn't cost much to live in Romania but when I came back to England I had to rely on my mother to buy me clothes. I'd even had to borrow one of my sister's outfits to wear to her own wedding.

All these thoughts felt like blasphemy. How dare I feel sorry for myself when my colleagues out there were giving up no less, and when we all had so much more than the people we were trying to help? I felt as if I was having to make a choice between my own life or the hundred Podriga residents, and I was deciding that I was more important. I kept crying as I tried to force myself to decide, hating myself for not being a better person, for not being prepared to give up everything. I talked endlessly to my mother about it, needing the approval of someone I respected, and she turned out to be surprisingly certain about what I should do. She saw me as already much too emotionally involved to be doing the job properly, and if I stayed out there much longer she reckoned I'd have little left to give. I was aware that my drive was going, that the constant battles and fighting to achieve every little change had worn me down. I was going to have to leave sometime, and there was no point in waiting till I was half-dead. I also knew that I was beginning to hate Romanians, to have a bitterness that meant I took all the knocks personally, and that was harmful to what we were trying to achieve out there. My travelling days when I'd loved them so much seemed a lifetime ago. Now I felt that the only people I cared about in that God-forsaken land were those locked inside the walls of Yonashen and Podriga. I'd had to be so hard in my dealings with those who held power over us that I was beginning to lose the very humanity that had driven me to help in the first place. What am I saying? Sometimes I felt that I was simply going mad out there, that it was such a weird country that I'd lost all sense of what was real. I knew that for my own good I should get out while the going was good, while there were still lots of other volunteers who cared about the place and would carry on the work with or without me. But there was so much more to do there – we'd only just started solving the problems, and I knew that I was needed. Yet if I stayed longer I would only make myself more indispensable, like Moona had become at Yonashen, where no one could conceive of operations running without him. I swung between feeling that I was probably being incredibly arrogant thinking that I was personally making much difference, and knowing that people were depending on me to make things happen.

My mother told me to set a date and stick to it. A chance

came for me to go and work in Africa and I decided to grab it. If I came back to France or England I knew that I was likely to sit and wallow in miserable guilt, but perhaps if I was in the real Third World I might decide that the Podriga residents had it lucky. I rang the others in Saveni and I told them that I was flying back the next week but I'd decided to leave for good in the middle of June. I felt that I was betraying them all, that I was dumping them all in it, leaving them to handle Marcan and all the official problems with their much-improved but still extremely rudimentary Romanian-language skills.

When I went back in May I expected them all to hate me as much as I was hating myself. But of course they didn't and it wasn't as bad as I expected. I was soon busy making arrangements for the huge water installations due to take place in August, and sorting out yet another passport crisis caused by the Botoshani police refusing to issue us with more visas. Hot weather had arrived suddenly, bringing its own set of problems as flies and maggots infested the toilet areas. Paddy and Robert were busy building a proper pathway between the two Podriga buildings, and Rob was taking the electricity up into the attic. There was never time to stop and think too much about my actual departure; now I simply had to get on with introducing Andrew, Aileen, Colette and Maureen to every contact I had in Saveni and Botoshani and doing all I could to ensure that my leaving wouldn't cause too many difficulties.

I confess to having been a coward with regard to telling the residents. I made up a story about a family crisis and said I had no choice about the decision. I just couldn't bring myself to tell them that I wanted to get on with my own life, that they didn't mean enough to me to make me want to stay forever. I felt that I was breaking a promise; we had told them since the start that we would stay until things were better, and now I was leaving when we'd only just begun.

D-day approached fast. Arranging export papers for

Hannibal and Georgie proved to be a much more complicated process than it had been when bringing them into Romania in the first place. I had to type out all the necessary papers myself since no one at the local office of the Ministry of Agriculture in Botoshani seemed to have a clue about what was needed. I arranged for Hannibal to have his tests for anaemia and glanders, and Georgie had another shot of rabies vaccine.

As was becoming usual, the Land Rover had all its lights and tyres pinched two days before we were due to set off. But perhaps it was a good thing, keeping me busy right up until the last minute, so I had very little time for goodbyes. The end was quite simply terrible. I only said goodbye to a few of the residents; I couldn't stop crying and it was upsetting us all too much. Even Sandina and Vasile, Podriga's horseman who'd been looking after Hannibal for the past six months, were crying, so finally I just tried to get away as quickly as possible. At Saveni we loaded up the Land Rover outside the apartment. Rob, the electrician, had finally decided to return to England and was driving home with me. Our stuff was packed, Hannibal was in the trailer behind and Georgie was positioned in her nest in the back. The final moment was a blur of tears and blazing bagpipes. Aileen came out on to the street blasting out 'Flower of Scotland'. I looked around at these friends, the other volunteers with whom I'd shared so much, and I realized I'd never known a more amazing group of people. I was going to miss them like hell.

Epilogue

I stayed in Africa much longer than I had originally planned. I saw much of the continent before taking up permanent work in Uganda, and it was October of the following year before I returned to Britain for a visit and had a chance to properly catch up with what had been going on in Romania since my departure. I travelled up to Scotland and had an emotional reunion with Maureen, Colette, Aileen and Andrew, all of whom had recently returned for good. Paddy was still out at Podriga with a new set of volunteers, carrying on what we had started. Speaking to him on the phone, it all came flooding back – the problems, though ever-changing, were essentially much the same.

The greatest physical change at Podriga since I had left was the water connection. The water team had come out from Britain in August, complete with seven kilometres of pipe, a digger, a Portakabin to live in that they were to leave with the volunteers at Podriga, and an enormous amount of enthusiasm. Complications were greater than any of us had predicted, however. The officials from Botoshani who had given us permission for the pipe route back in April suddenly decided that a different path must be taken through Saveni, involving the digging up of tarmac for which the British team had not brought out equipment. GOSCOM had not yet acquired the fixtures they had promised for attaching our pipes to their Saveni water station. High rainfall meant that the ground was extraordinarily boggy so the actual laying of the pipe through the open land between Saveni and Podriga was much harder than expected. The sides of the trenches dug would collapse without people actually standing in them to hold them up until the pipe was in and placed correctly. Once the team reached the village of Podriga there were yet more problems as villagers realized that for the pipes to be laid beneath the wide ditches at the side of the road, they would have to take down the little foot bridges that led to their front gates. They reacted with unprecedented antagonism and came out with shovels and pitch forks to stop further progress. Three days of negotiations were necessary before the waterboys were allowed to proceed.

Finally at Podriga the hospital was reached. GOSCOM made the connection at Saveni, the tap was switched on, and . . . nothing. Checks were made for blockages, leaks, cracks . . . until the only answer remaining was that the engineer from Botoshani had got his sums wrong. Gravity was not enough to draw the water from the hill in Saveni, and a pump would be needed.

The waterboys went home and the Scottish office set about raising more funds. A pump eventually arrived and was fitted, hopes were high, and out came the first promising splutters. Splutters was all it was, however. GOSCOM had not connected us to a twenty-four hour supply as they had promised, but just switched the taps on at sporadic intervals. The distance between Saveni and Podriga meant that each time this happened hours of bleeding were necessary. The pump couldn't cope with this, and Podriga was back to square one.

It was over a year before all these problems were finally solved, but solved they were and at last Podriga enjoys a full water supply. Each resident now has at least two hot baths a week and filthy toilets are a nightmare of the past. A new laundry – the latest fund-raising project – can now be installed, probably out in the grounds at the back of the building.

The Portakabin brought out by the waterboys stayed and became a common room, a safe haven where the residents can draw and read, and where the volunteers can give them one-to-one attention that isn't possible in the shared rooms of the main building. A small barn was built by the volunteers for the fuel, so now wood and coal is kept dry, can be chopped in all weathers, and is safe from the thieving hands of certain villagers.

The outside of the building has been replastered and looks a great deal better, although I'm not sure about the colour – it was painted a rather extraordinary pink. Inside there is still a long way to go. Recent photographs are depressing, for many could have been taken soon after our arrival. But if the physical changes at Podriga have not come as quickly as we had hoped, this hides the incredible change in attitudes that has occurred, and maybe in the long run it is better that it has happened this way round. Their surroundings may not have changed a great deal as yet, but the general depression that hung over both residents and staff has lifted. As I spoke to Maureen, to Andrew, to Aileen and Colette and all the other volunteers who had recently returned from Podriga, the same fact kept hitting me: that the co-operation and goodwill they had finally found from the Romanian staff was achieving far more than any hot bath or replastered wall. The really rotten eggs remained, of course: Headlice is as antagonistic as ever, Marcan and others just as hostile – but the fat sisters and most of the care workers have become allies. Perhaps this happened just from the sheer staying power of the volunteers: however nasty they were, we simply wouldn't go away, so maybe they decided they might as well help us. But more importantly they have been inspired by two brave Romanians who have been kicking at the system from within.

At around the time I was leaving, I met at Psychy Number Four in Botoshani a very quiet and well-mannered doctor named Chimpavu. He had been to Podriga and expressed his great admiration for what we were doing there. He then said that he and his wife, also a psychiatric doctor, would like to help. I spoke to them both and discussed with them the plans that we had for Podriga, but at the time I did not see much then that they could do as junior and therefore relatively powerless doctors from Botoshani.

The next spring, however, they came up trumps. They obtained permission to come and work at Podriga for three months. As doctors they had authority over Headlice and the Podriga medical assistants – and they used it. They came and they 'kicked ass', achieving far more than we ever could as foreigners trying to fight the system from without. Every resident was X-rayed for TB, and all those in need of treatment sent for specialist care. The drug abuse was finally controlled, with those in need of medication being put on regular, recorded doses. The old guy in charge of collecting food and fuel supplies was sacked for theft; care workers were fined for mistreating residents in the Pavilion; medical assistants weren't allowed to sit around in the staff room all day. Headlice's private stores were finally taken away from him, freeing two extra rooms for the residents and scoring an important psychological victory.

The Chimpavus suffered repercussions, of course. Their overriding of the Saveni management's authority led to some devious attempts at having them removed, and they have probably done terrible damage to their future careers. But they were a true inspiration to the Podriga staff, residents and volunteers; they were gentle and patient with the residents themselves, yet determined to do more than just bring comfort – to ring changes. They proved that lack of funds was not the sole cause of Podriga's ills: and this, it seems, cemented the change in attitude of the staff, by helping them to realize that they *did* have the power to change things themselves. Marishika is now to be seen yelling down the phone to Saveni with her demands for supplies – gone are the days when she would just repeat '*nu e posible*' when we asked her to do something for us. The doctors Chimpavu still visit, and they also brought in the help of the GP from Dragoshen, the small town on the other side of Podriga, who is working with new volunteer nurses to establish regular health care. He comes almost every day and is popular with the staff; he is prepared to fight Saveni when need be, and his long-term commitment gives great hope for lasting changes.

There has recently been a fantastic breakthrough at the administrative level regarding Podriga's future. Since the time of our arrival we had been fighting to remove Podriga from the authority of Saveni Hospital, and for it to become a separate unit within the Health Ministry or else move to the authority of the Ministry for the Handicapped. The Scottish office of the charity had even brought the matter up in Brussels at the EC, and my father had continued correspondence with the Ministry of Health in Bucharest in an attempt to give the request some political clout. At last it is being taken up, and independence is scheduled for January 1994. Podriga will be given its own director – hopefully one of the Chimpavus or the Dragoshen doctor will be persuaded to take up the post – and will receive its own funds and supplies. The possible benefits are immeasurable, and the volunteers currently at Podriga are filled with great hope.

Over at Yonashen, the volunteer story is nearly over. The Romanians are at last coping well on their own and just three volunteers remain to oversee some building projects and make sure all runs smoothly. Last year had its problems, with Gushu turning particularly nasty and refusing to sanction new volunteer changes, but conditions for the children have continued to steadily improve. There are now eight medical assistants, Romanian physiotherapists, and a full-time Romanian doctor. *Triaj* had a full face-lift, with a new toilet and bathing area and all the plaster in its rooms taken back to the brick and replastered and painted. The *Triaj* staff are now amongst the most enthusiastic, and it is no longer the forgotten section at the back of the building. A tarmac playground was built in the grounds, and a fantastic huge wooden treehouse has been created by Henry. A large greenhouse was put up next to the rehab unit, so Yonashen now has its very own tomatoes and salads in the summer.

In the Front Section, Fiona succeeded in having the younger children's mental abilities reassessed. Eight were reclassified as normal, and they were moved to an orphanage in Botoshani where they now receive proper schooling. It is a clean, happy place, with highly motivated Romanian care staff and teachers, so with fingers crossed we are hoping that they have a chance of leading a normal life. Amongst them is Gabriella, much smaller than any of the other children and still refusing to eat anything but the bread and milk that Susan weaned her on to, but she seems happy and is talking well.

The more capable older children, Florin amongst them, spend their days in the village with Romanian families in a project that has been highly successful. About ten families agreed to take them on, and by helping around the house or out with the animals, they are learning the skills of life that most children take for granted.

And finally, Blondu. As tends to happen with fairy tales, they don't really work out in real life. His family couldn't cope with him and after a year he returned to Yonashen. Understandably, he was extremely unhappy at first and was moody and difficult. But his naturally cheerful character soon emerged and once again he is a central figure of Yonashen life, charming any new volunteers and remaining a favourite amongst the staff. He spends most of his days in the village, and I hear that he is really trying to speak now. There is talk of sending him to a special deaf school, so maybe there could be a happy ending after all . . .

I've been asked to go back to Romania for a week or so to write 'the final chapter'. I'm refusing, however, because emotionally I know that I couldn't cope with it. To go back as an observer, without being able to help, probably just getting in the way of the volunteers now out there, would drive me crazy with frustration. And then to have to leave, to have to say a final goodbye to the Yonashen children and the Podriga residents all over again . . . Leaving Romania was the hardest thing I've ever had to do, and to do it again would be more than I could bear.